YORKSHIRE:
THE DALES

For Anne and Peter

YORKSHIRE: THE DALES

Maurice Colbeck

B. T. BATSFORD LTD

LONDON

First published 1979
© Maurice Colbeck 1979
Photoset by Photobooks (Bristol) Ltd.
28/30 Midland Road, St. Philips, Bristol
and printed in Great Britain by
Redwood Burn Ltd., Trowbridge and Esher
for the publishers B. T. Batsford Ltd.,
4 Fitzhardinge Street, London W1H 0AH

ISBN 0 7134 2236 X

CONTENTS

Acknowledgments   6
List of Illustrations   7
Map of The Dales   8
Foreword   11

Introduction: England's Heart and Backbone   13

1 Malhamdale and Airedale –   20
   A River born in mystery

2 Ribblesdale to Dentdale –   34
   A Touch of Carlislitis

3 Valley of the Wharfe –   50
   'Classic' of the Dales

4 Haunted Dale of Nidd –   80
   T'Owd Man's Kingdom

5 Wensleydale –   103
   Ripon to Lonely Lunds

6 Swaledale to Teesdale –   136
   A Diversity of Treasures

Bibliography   156
Index   157

ACKNOWLEDGMENTS

The Author and Publishers would like to thank the following for permission to reproduce the photographs in this book:
L. and M. Gayton, nos 1, 11, 12; A. F. Kersting, nos 10, 13, 14, 19, 22, 23, 25, 26; K. Scowen, nos 7, 24; J. Smithson, no. 6; D.G. Widdicombe, nos 2, 3, 4, 5, 8, 15, 16, 17, 27. Photographs nos 9, 18, 20, 21 were taken by the late Noel Habgood and are from D. G. Widdicombe's collection. The map is by Patrick Leeson.

ILLUSTRATIONS

Plates   *Between pages 48-49*
1 Thwaite
2 Dales Farm, Capon Hall, near Malham Tarn
3 Rocks at Malham Cove
4 Brant Fell
5 The Sun Inn at Dent Town
6 Ingleborough
7 The Ribble at Stainforth Bridge
8 Arncliffe

Between pages 96-97

9 Harewood House
10 Bolton Priory
11 Burnsall
12 Hubberholme Church
13 Harrogate
14 Knaresborough Castle
15 Catrake Force
16 Penhill

Between pages 128-129

17 Hardraw Force
18 Masham
19 Ripon Cathedral
20 Middleham Castle
21 Fountains Abbey
22 Nappa Hall
23 Snape Castle
24 Muker
25 Easby Church
26 Easby Abbey
27 Richmond

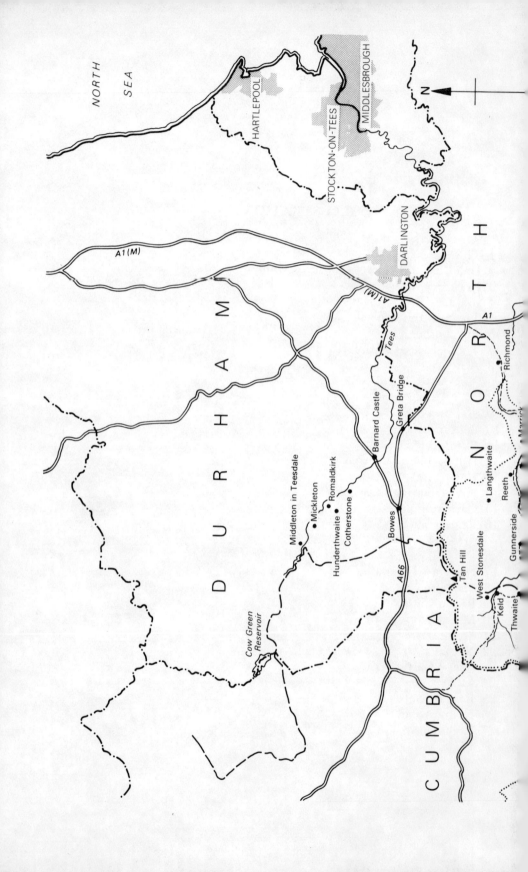

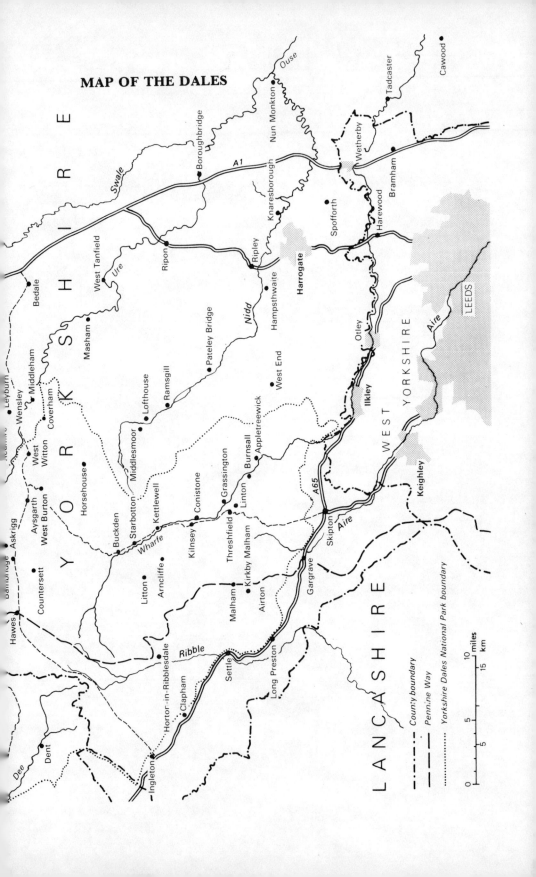

MAP OF THE DALES

Foreword

The Dales which are the subject of this book are the Pennine Dales in that part of North-west Yorkshire which is largely included in the Yorkshire Dales National Park. However, since some areas of great beauty and interest are unaccountably (to me) excluded from the National Park, I have made my choice from a wider area and have wandered as the fancy took me over the new county boundaries, imposed in 1974, into what is now considered part of Durham or Cumbria.

Even the Dales undergo change, and no doubt by the time this book appears, some of my facts will have been falsified by events. If so, I hope my readers will be tolerant. I hope, too, to be excused in cases, if any, where copyright may have been unknowingly infringed.

I am grateful to many people for their generous help with information – the proprietors of Skipton Castle, the editor of the *Craven Herald and Pioneer*, Dr and Mrs Peter Annison, Mr Kit Calvert of Hawes, to mention only a few. Some of the numerous books which have proved most useful are listed in a bibliography. Special thanks are due to Geoffrey N. Wright, who read the proofs. Remaining errors are my own.

Most of all I am indebted as always to the untiring help and encouragement of my long-suffering wife.

England's Heart and Backbone

Native loyalties apart, most Yorkshiremen, I would think, look to the Dales as the essential Yorkshire: they have a foot in both the North Riding and the West; they have mountains and consequent waterfalls; their exposed limestone scars produce a dramatic scenery rarely surpassed in any part of Britain. Fantastic, weathered outcrops create in places a natural statuary which might have been the work of Henry Moore (small wonder that, being a Yorkshireman, he once told me that the shapes of rocks in his native countryside were among the formative influences of his art).

Underground, too, there is nowhere quite like the Dales, where huge, cathedral-like caverns, vast and mysterious networks of streams and passages provide an ancestral home for a highly superior race of boggarts – recognised with delight, when I tried to describe them to a friend from the Baltic coast, as – *'Trolls!'*

The Dales have castles and abbeys, villages and churches of rare beauty; they have market towns whose bustle is in colourful contrast with the quietude of lonely farms lost in seemingly endless miles of rolling moorland, and they have, too, the ruins not only of abbeys and castles, but of past industry – lead mines and mills, melting slowly but inexorably back into the fabric of the fells.

More and more people travel farther and farther to see them, but the Dales, it seems to me, remain not only 'unspoiled' but – quite often – truly *improved.*

Perhaps one reason they have remained so largely unsullied must be an almost incredible ignorance of their attractions – an ignorance that remained widespread until the dawn of the Great Car Age; and fortunately, before that could do too much damage, rescue was at hand: the Yorkshire Dales National Park was designated in 1954 and is administered with great energy and responsibility by the Yorkshire Dales National Park Committee of the North Yorkshire County Council.

Even where the mark of the car *has* despoiled the Dales, the damage is not irrevocable and it *is* being remedied. Brimham Rocks, near Pateley Bridge, not long ago saw the provision of new facilities at what had been a favourite Dales 'beauty spot' since the eighteenth century. Here, the National Trust, with the co-operation of the Countryside Commission, has reversed the destructive trend of human erosion. As Lord Winstanley, chairman of the Commission, said, they have safeguarded this long-established part of our Yorkshire heritage for our children and for their children. Before that development, cars parking at the feet of Brimham's stone fantasies – like the Idol Rock and the Dancing Bear, the Oyster Shell and the Druid's Writing Desk – had virtually killed the grass and made the place rather resemble a car dump designed by Salvador Dali!

The Dales are no longer as isolated as once they were, though those to whom they are only a name can have little idea of the immensity of their great spaces. A southerner told me recently, with some surprise, that he considered Yorkshire's moorlands excelled those of the West Country. There is a satisfaction, sometimes, in being told what you have always known, but on that occasion it was tinged with misgiving – because the more people visit them, the less will the Dales remain the refuge of peace and beauty we so much love.

Fortunately, the National Park Committee has so far withstood any temptation to 'sell' the Dales by catering for the requirements of every possible visitor. They recognize that visitors are transients; that the Dales have a life independent of these casual callers and that it matters enormously that this essential life should be safeguarded. And surely, if the Dales existed only for visiting they would hardly be worth it! Happily – dare I say it – not everyone loves the Dales! People fond of funfairs and bedazzled by big hotels, and bright lights generally, would be bored there.

Yet, thankful, as I am for the existence of the Dales National Park, I rather fail to understand why it excludes Nidderdale, Teesdale and parts of Ribblesdale, which are among my own best-loved areas. One of us most be wrong! But it hardly matters which, because my readers will find it a delightful task to investigate and decide for themselves.

What *are* the Dales: how do they differ from the many other areas of natural beauty in the British Isles? Essentially, they are valleys – the word 'dale' in fact is derived from the Old Norse word *Dalr* – and they were formed in the Ice Age by glaciers which ground relentlessly along the existing river courses, scouring away the softer rock and soil so that the original V of the valley became a U, with the almost perfectly flat bottom and steep sides which create some of the most beautiful prospects in the Dales today.

At the same time the glaciers carried great rocks and other debris to scatter them around in certain areas, such as Norber, where a remarkable collection of such 'erratics', many of them several tons in weight, rests on the south side of Ingleborough, above Austwick in Ribblesdale. Of Silurian slate, many rest on plinths of the carboniferous limestone from an earlier period, which forms their 'platform'.

The glaciers also formed tarns and what has been called 'the only lake in the Dales' – Semerwater – by scooping out hollows and blocking river outlets with their debris. But when the glaciers melted, Yorkshire's own 'lake district' largely disappeared, leaving 'dry valleys' where they had overflowed. You will find the most famous one above Malham Cove: it is an eerie feeling to walk along the stony bed of this dry and desolate valley, where once a river rushed and gurgled.

When the glaciers had passed, the Dales became green again, as first moss and grass and, later, trees appeared. Reindeer herds, and nomads who lived upon them, knew these hills and valleys. Later still, about 3000 BC, other people settled to grow grain on the lower slopes of the hills; to make simple pottery and leave behind tools of flint and hardstone and the barrows where they laid their dead.

The Bronze Age came and went, leaving its mark in stone circles at Yockenthwaite and Appletreewick in Wharfedale; at Carperby in Wensleydale. Colder, wetter weather drove many eastward towards the Plain of York; though hardy souls elected to settle in the highlands. Something less than a thousand years later, Yorkshire acquired a Celtic culture as Iron Age man reached northern England to share the Dales with a proud native tribe, the Brigantes.

The Romans – who found the Brigantes a.hard nut to crack – left small mark upon the Dales; though they mined lead in Nidderdale and Swaledale (using native slave labour), built forts and, of course, made roads. But the cold and doubtless hostile uplands were less to their taste than they were to such later invaders as the Angles from Germany, who, having reached the Vale of York by way of the Ouse, established the Anglian kingdom of Northumbria. And these vigorous, pioneering people, who tilled the soil and kept sheep and cattle and pigs, were to make the deepest mark so far of any visitors to the Dales, clearing the woodland and building churches and monasteries – for instance, that at Ripon, founded by St Wilfrid in 660.

But while Anglian peasants listened in docility to the missionaries who stood beneath their preaching crosses, dragon-prowed ships were sailing from Denmark. Their fierce, fair-haired warriors conquered York and they became rulers of the North. But Yorkshire seems finally to have tamed even them! They mingled easily with the Anglian people, so like themselves, and cultivated the lower Dales areas.

Later invaders, Norsemen who came to England via Ireland, preferred the higher lands, wherein to live a life little different from that of their Norwegian homeland, grazing their cattle on hill shielings in the summer and moving them into the valleys during spring and autumn. The Norsemen left their mark in the language of the Dales, too, with words like *thwaite*, meaning a field or clearing, which now we find in names like Hampsthwaite and Yockenthwaite and Thwaite, the Swaledale village, itself.

Then – for many disastrously – came the Normans to make the greatest impact of all and to mould the Dales into the form we largely see today. They set aside forest land for hunting; they brought in their monks to found abbeys and practise the sheep-breeding that is still an integral part of Dales life. The monks mined lead, too, burned charcoal, and built the first stone walls. Today, their ruined monasteries – at Fountains and Jervaulx, Bolton Abbey, Coverham and Easby – still play their part in Dales life, if only as historic enhancements of the scenery.

Walls are the mark of the Dales – a tracery, often irregular, of drystone boundaries sometimes of shining white limestone, which patterns the fells. The enclosing of the land began in the sixteenth century. And not only the monks built walls – villagers, too, fenced off with stone the land surrounding their homes. And in later years the process was continued by farmers and landowners.

Man restores, in some ages, what earlier men have taken away. For centuries the woodlands had been plundered for timber. Now Kingsley's friend, Walter Morrison, of Malham, planted trees by the thousand, with varying degrees of success. Since, today, the Forestry Commission is putting back in some ways what man took away, and in the original forest areas, too, I find it difficult to resent the process. But then, to me a tree can hardly ever be out of place: nor, for that matter, can the beauty of water. I sometimes wonder whether the reservoirs of Nidderdale have debarred it from inclusion in the National Park area. Yet surely that dale would be poorer without the spacious glitter of Gouthwaite and the wealth of life it has lured from meek moorhen to lordly eagle. . . . And after all, the Dales were a lakeland once, long ago. Whether or not you feel that water fits comfortably into the Dales setting, few would dispute that Semerwater is a jewel snugly set in its surrounding hills. No question, of course, that *this* legend-haunted water is the unassisted work of nature.

Buildings, of course, the man-made scenery of the Dales, are either in harmony or discord with their surroundings. Here, as perhaps nowhere else, houses, farms and churches seem to have grown out of the stuff of the fells, almost as if man had never been involved. Look at Muker in Swaledale, with grey houses climbing the hillside, or its near neighbour Thwaite: they seem, if anything, more 'naturally' a part of the landscape than some of nature's own extravagances in the way of limestone outcrops, gigantic stone gargoyles of erosion, or glacier-scattered boulders.

Men built with what they had in plenty – and that was stone – whether they were raising castles, churches, houses or barns. They laboured according to long-established pattern, well knowing that the weather in winter would beat upon their building with a penetrating ferocity seldom found elsewhere, but that their work would abide as indeed it does today, to become what they never dreamed – an indispensable part of the attraction of the Dales.

What of the people inhabiting those houses and congregating, even today, in those churches? Are they, in fact, noticeably different from people anywhere else in the country, despite attempts to caricature them as a race apart?

Being first and last Yorkshiremen, they probably believe (and might even tell you) that they *are* a race apart. And perhaps the folk-belief that Yorkshiremen are 'different' is not without some foundation. But there are *varieties* even of Yorkshiremen! The less attractive type of West Riding millionaire (if he really exists), caricatured as an insensitive, grasping self-made man who whole-heartedly approves his own way of life, no matter what the rest of the world may think of it, might be hardly at home in the Dales (perhaps because the Dales would be more than equal to dealing with him). Yet one of the characteristics that mark him most strongly – a love of independence – is very much in evidence in north-west Yorkshire. Dalesmen are not so much a proud people, as unshakeable in their determination to be, first and last, *themselves.*

There are always exceptions, of course, but if I dare generalise, Dalesmen (and that goes for women, too) are inclined to drive hard bargains in business, though that is a thing quite apart from the absolute obligation they feel to offer generous hospitality to strangers; even if those strangers are so ill-advised as to consider the Dalesman – at first sight – a slow-witted rustic. In fact (as they will probably soon discover) he is extremely quick-witted, enjoying nothing so much as a verbal contest which he usually takes great delight in winning!

Few men have understood the Dalesman's nature better than R.W.S. Bishop, a doctor for many years in Wensleydale. Not only did he gain the confidence of his often difficult patients, but – perhaps even more remarkable – he usually won their acquiescence in whatever treatments he considered to be for their best good.

During the last years of his life he wrote a book, *My Moorland Patients*, a classic of its kind, which was first published in 1922, the year after his death and subsequent burial in Tanfield churchyard beside his beloved Ure. (It has been republished as *Moorland Doctor.*)

The Yorkshire Dales that Bishop describes existed before the First World War, and even then, he reported sadly: 'Life and character on the moorland, is rapidly changing. With the coming of the motor-car and cycle, the charm and seclusion of remote England has nearly departed. No far-off moorland lane is now free from their intrusion, and it is fortunate that they cannot yet jump the stone walls and hedges so that the footpaths are still left to us. What it will be like when the air is thick with flying machines, I will not attempt to imagine.'

Happily, Dr Bishop's worst fears were not realised. There are certainly far more cars than he would remember, but they have still to learn to jump the hedges; and as cars have increased in number, so have the car parks, a feature which may well have been unheard of in the Dales he knew. Nor, even today, are the Dales skies quite 'thick with flying machines'.

Despite Bishop's lamentations for the 'old kindly hospitality . . . the disappearance of countless old words' and a limitation of 'the frequency and fierceness of the old Yorkshire bargainings', I think his book has more than a purely historical value, for the Dalesman of today is very much a descendant of the people Bishop describes, and anyone who spends much time in a Dales schoolroom or listens to a Yorkshire teacher's account of his pupils will have little doubt that the old quickness of wit and directness of speech is still very much in evidence in the youngest generation of Dalesfolk.

Here is one of the doctor's most revealing stories: it shows the Dalesman's determination not to yield to petty dictatorship; his decisiveness in action; his mastery of economy in verbal communication – and gives a useful, if small, sample of Dales dialect. (I shall not attempt to translate, as it'll 'appen prove more educational to let t' reader sooart it out for hissen.)

A Dalesman's aged uncle had died in a distant workhouse. After some unavoidable delay, the nephew called on the vicar to make the funeral arrangements – only to be kept hanging about longer than suited his temper. He addressed the reverend gentleman thus: 'Noo then, we s'all bring t' aud lad ten miles by t' road, an' we reckon we s'all be at t' chetch by three by t' clock or rather mair for t' sahding termorrow arterean'.

The vicar, rather nettled, retorted that his own convenience had to be considered and 'You cannot have funerals just when you think fit'.

Further haggling found the parties no closer to agreement.

'I'll warrant thee', the Dalesman retorted, 'we s'all bring t' aud lad along in his box, an' if thou weean't hap t' job up, then we s'all upend him ageean t'chetch door, an' thou can sahd him whenever thou's amind'. The funeral took place at three o'clock next afternoon without further ado.

Speak of the Dales – in whatever dialect – and you speak of England. The main Dales rivers (if not the wayward Ribble which defects to Lancashire) run from their birthplace, England's watershed, towards

York, once Eoforwic, a capital of the Vikings like those who found the Dales a homeland long ago. York's history, said King George VI, was that of England itself, and, for many who know them, the Dales are not only Yorkshire's backbone and heartland, but perhaps England's, too.

ONE

Malhamdale and Airedale

A River born in mystery

If I had to recommend any part of the Dales to a foreign visitor whose time was too short to take in more, I would offer him Malhamdale, confident that the memories he would take from this birthplace of the Aire would be more sharply etched, more deeply impressed than those from many another visit to many another dale.

For where else could you find that is offered here in such a little compass? Malham Cove would be enough of a natural spectacle for any dale, but here it is most aggressively rivalled by another consequence of the mid-Craven fault – Gordale Scar. In the Yorkshire Dales, any sizeable stretch of water is a novelty, yet Malhamdale nonchalantly presents us with Malham Tarn, the largest natural lake in the West Riding, fully equal in interest and attraction to that only other famous Dales lake, Semerwater.

There is history, too, in Malhamdale and echoes of literature and memories of great names; but the stirring and violent tales are part of a dream now, as cattle, horses and a black cat on the roadside verge at Calton sleep in the sun. For if peace was what my foreigner sought he could hardly find it deeper than in villages like Otterburn, Calton, Winterburn and Hetton. Yet the sequestered calm of villages which appear to be set in the clefts of great limestone rocks is in sharp contrast with the wildness of the bleak and desolate uplands.

Rock . . . rock . . . rock. That, surely would be my visitor's most abiding impression; and whether the limestone of Malhamdale is really whiter than that in any other dale I do not know – but it certainly seems so to my eyes.

In most of the chapters that follow, I trace our Dales rivers to their source, but the Aire, with her dramatic and mysterious origins, calls for different treatment.

For all her spectacular and lyrical start in life, Yorkshire's river of industry is sadly sullied before she ends her long journey. She first loses her innocence by industrial dalliance with Keighley; she is not completely lost as she traverses Bingley and Saltaire (where the

Victorian Nonconformist millowner Sir Titus Salt makes a final bid for her good character by giving her name to the pub-less model village created on her banks for his workers). Alas, despite his redemptive efforts the brash appeal of prosperous Leeds proves irresistible. So, sensing that Bradford will have her if he can, she neatly evades his embraces. But even Leeds cannot hold her! Perhaps already she hears the call of the distant sea. At Castleford she is joined by her incurably working-class sister Calder and together they cross the low-lying lands south of Selby to meet the Ouse, and flow with her to join the Humber and run away to sea.

During her wayward course she has left her name on three places, Airton, Saltaire and Airmyn – all so diverse that they might belong to different countries rather than the course of one river – even a river that crosses almost the entire West Riding.

But if the story of the Aire demands to begin at the river's Malhamdale birthplace, can we find that with any certainty? Is the Aire *really* born in Malham Tarn? It is generally thought so, but there are problems, for the stream which runs from the Tarn towards the crescent cliffs of Malham Cove now vanishes underground at Water Sinks, several hundred yards after leaving the Tarn. At one time it flowed as a continuous river to Malham Cove to pour over the lip of the 300-foot limestone face before plunging down – a thrilling sight, surely, for whoever was there to see it.

Now a stream, long thought to be the infant Aire, emerges from the foot of the Cove – but it has been proved by experiments with dyes that the rivulet from Malham Tarn, last seen at Water Sinks, emerges not here, but at Aire Head Springs below Malham; whereas the stream we see issuing from the foot of the Cove began life high on Malham Moor. South-West of the Tarn, near a disused smelt mill, it, too, disappeared to emerge as we see it here. Where, then, does the Aire begin?

In times of flood water from the Tarn unquestionably reaches the Aire Head Springs more quickly than it gets to this stream which flows from the foot of the Cove. So what is the explanation? Some have postulated the existence behind the Cove of ponderous natural machinery in the form of a huge syphoning system or the presence of high, hidden waterfalls with cavernous pools feeding the stream from the Cove, while the water from Tarn to Springs takes a straighter and therefore quicker route.

One man, at least, thought he knew the answer, but until his findings are proved true or false we are unlikely to know precisely what his theory is – though we do know in part.

That reverend gentleman, popularly called the 'Spooky Parson' (but officially the Revd. Charles L. Tweedale, of Weston Vicarage, near Otley) claimed in 1932 that the secret of Malham Cove had been revealed to him by the spirits of the dead. His predictions, he claimed, would be verified in due course when someone explored what lay behind the 300-foot limestone face of the Cove. He wrote down his forecasts and sealed them in an envelope which he gave to the then chairman of Malham Parish Meeting.

Today, that chairman's successor still holds the envelope with its seals intact, for nobody has yet penetrated either the Cove or its mystery. Mr Tweedale's theories, as far as we know them, are a little disappointing, perhaps, as the result of such unusual communications. His spirit friends were obliging and thorough, not to say gifted! One of them, called Tabitha, wrote, or dictated, in verse and guided the vicar's hand in drawing sketches of tunnels and submerged pools. The secret of the Cove seems to have been an obsession with him and he clashed with the local Parish Meeting, who objected, understandably, to his proposal to dynamite the face of the Cove and make a tunnel!

He believed that behind the Cove there was a vast underground lake – which is not unreasonable, for the flow from the foot of the Cove is constantly strong, regardless of the weather.

Utterly determined, he proposed an assault by young enthusiasts. Having hidden their tools previously by night in the trees, so as to avoid discovery, they would lower the stream and thus be able to unmask the secret of the Cove before anyone could see them and interfere. Happily, perhaps, the best-laid plans came to nothing. Since his day, caving and underwater exploration have progressed and several more promising attempts have been made to discover the secret. But still the seals on the 'Spooky Parson's' letter remain unbroken.· . . .

Malham Tarn may not boast a monster on the Loch Ness pattern but it hardly needs one. Its waters on their bed of Silurian slate cover 150 acres and are contained by the debris left by a glacier. Once it belonged to Walter Morrison, the millionaire friend of Charles Kingsley, who stayed at Tarn House (Morrison's 'mountain home' among oak woods on the Tarn's north side) while he was writing *The Water Babies*. Charles Darwin, too, was a friend of the well-connected Mr Morrison, and his scientific shade doubtless approves the use to which Tarn House is put today by the Field Studies Council, who lease it from the National Trust.

I can easily imagine Darwin giving his respected opinion on a peculiarity of the Malham Tarn trout, which for some reason had a deficiency in the gill cover (or operculum). Perhaps it was caused by something in the moorland water, for when a former owner of the estate, Thomas Lister (later the first Lord Ribblesdale), introduced fish from Loch Leven they acquired the same defect. I wonder if the monks of Fountains Abbey, who once owned the fishery, noticed and wondered at the same singularity.

Had he lived late enough, Darwin might have been made an honorary member of the Yorkshire Naturalists' Trust, one of whose nature reserves is Globe Flower Wood, a mile west of the Tarn. This beautiful half-acre is enclosed by a limestone wall, over which visitors are encouraged to look at flowers, most of them best seen in June. The wall prevents the risk of damage to such marsh meadow beauties as the globe flower, wood cranesbill, wood anemones and *Cirsium heterophyllum*, the poor 'melancholy thistle'. Trees, too – sycamore, birch and alder – grow in the damp, brown earth, flushed from time to time with lime-rich water.

Some would say that trees were hardly at home here in this strange landscape, almost 'lunar' (but for its grass) dotted and pitted with outcropping limestone. But strolling over his domain, the millionaire of Tarn House had the idea that trees might improve the bare limestone landscape of Malham Moor, so he planted a million of them, of which about 50,000 still maintain a struggling life.

The Pennine Way snakes round the northern and eastern sides of the Tarn, crossing Malham Lings and turning westward at Sheriff Hill to skirt the Cove. By some, whose ignorance must be forgiven on geographical grounds, Malham Cove has been mistaken for a quarry. *Some quarriers* they would need to be to have carved this gigantic natural stage-set which gleams white on fine days as the sunlight flashes from its limestone cliff.

Eighteenth-century tourists revelled in the awesomeness of Malham-dale's sights – particularly the Cove and Gordale Scar. And how they exaggerated! One said the Cove was twice the height of Niagara and that over it, in times of flood, poured a stupendous cataract. Ruskin and Kingsley, on strolls from Tarn House, paid it due tribute and Kingsley was quick to make use of it in *The Water Babies*.

Such visitors were still more impressed by Gordale Scar, a mile or so to the east (but best reached from Malham village). It was 'dreadful', 'horrid' and of course 'stupendous'. They entered the great roofless cave (a fair and no doubt accurate description) with the exciting sensation of grasshoppers about to be crushed. The cold drops which still surprise visitors as they fall on them with no small force were to them like giant drops of sweat. We are less theatrical today in our appreciation of natural scenery, but we can hardly be blasé about Gordale Scar even now.

Turner, Gray and Wordsworth came here and recorded their impressions in words or paint. Wordsworth saw William Westall's painting of the Scar and found the mere picture inspiration enough for a sonnet.

Gray made his pilgrimage in 1769 on a gloomy October day that he considered enhanced the savage aspects of the place. He learned that the inn at Malham where he dined had lately given hospitality to three landscape painters with the same destination – John 'Warwick' Smith, François Vivares and William Bellers.

Gordale's is a durable magic. More than 40 years later, James Ward, who was born in the year of Gray's visit, finished his huge painting *A Landscape, Gordale Scar, Yorkshire.* Measuring 131 by 166 inches, it hangs now in the Tate Gallery. Ward may well have been right in recognising the need for a big enough canvas for such a subject and it could certainly be claimed that his version is among the most impressive (if not quite the most accurate).

It was inevitable, I suppose, that the greatest of them all, Turner, should be commissioned by his host Walter Farnley, to draw the Scar while he was staying a mere boulder-toss away at Farnley Hall, Otley (where some of his pictures are still to be seen). The Leeds artist John William Inchbold painted the Scar in 1876 – and so the tradition goes on, maintained in our own day by John Piper and doubtless many other courageous if less distinguished souls whose work will never be seen by visitors to the Tate.

You approach the Scar across a field through which wind the courses of streams, some empty, but for white limestone boulders, and others in which the water is green with cresses. At first glance the Scar looks like a solid barrier of rock, higher and more darkly threatening, with its cliffs 380 feet high, than Malham Cove. As you scramble closer over the rough, rocky floor, the cliffs become more precipitous, the chasm narrows, then suddenly, as you turn a corner you may see Gordale Beck plunging down in a waterfall. The sight, after heavy rain, must have been enough to inspire those enthusiastic early tourists to unprecedented eloquence.

The first impression on looking at the main face of the rock is that in the middle is a huge fossilised tree-root. It is, in fact, a fine example of tufa – volcanic rock with a glazed and rippled surface.

And so back to Malham, passing Janet's Cave and Foss (a Norse word for waterfall) on the way.

'Malham? It's the biggest open-air schoolroom in England', said the man I met at lunch at Beck Hall, in a low room whose walls were embellished with paintings of Cove and Scar, as well as an assortment of weapons and, at one end, richly carved dark oak. It all looked so ancient that I asked when the hall was built. The present building, I was told, dated largely from two hundred years ago but there had been a house on the site since about 1500. 'It's been messed about a lot.'

Through the window I could see a mallard escorting her progeny about the beck from which this hall (that you must cross a bridge to reach) takes its name. I wished no worse 'messing about' had ever taken place in a Yorkshire village. . . .

Close to Beck Hall, the monks of Fountains Abbey had the ancient equivalent of a medieval estate office to deal with their business in the sheep they 'ran' from here up to Malham Moor and beyond (as well as breeding famous horses at Bordley, east of Gordale Scar). In those days, at shearing time, the peace you can still find in modern, mid-week Malham would be unknown – bleated away by sheep in their thousands. Hereabouts, too, were the ewes whose milk went to make Dales cheese of a delectable quality hard to find today. But dismiss from your mind images of desirable dairymaids decorating the milking stands. For the canons whose tables they served protected themselves from temptation by employing only the old and the ugly.

Fortunately, no such ban applies today, for Malham is pre-eminently a place for youth. Besides the thousands of schoolchildren and students who visit the 'open-air classroom', Youth Hostellers and Pennine Way walkers abound. They trickle constantly through the information centre, with its relief maps and models demonstrating the geological eccentricities of the area; they visit the gift shop (inevitable in a place like Malham, yet as unobtrusive as they manage to keep such things in the Dales); and stream out on to the moorlands, criss-crossed by dry-stone walls and peppered by outcropping limestone.

Malham, one of the most popular of Pennine centres, is best visited, perhaps, on a sparkling December day. But now it is June, and if the great monastic sheep-runs are no more, it is still necessary to exhibit notices warning us to keep our dogs under control, for there are lambs about. It is haytime, too, so other posters remind us that the meadow grass, so pleasant to walk upon, is next year's fodder for sheep and cattle. They ask us to keep to the paths and walk in single file.

Like Scarborough and Harrogate, Malham is especially dear to Yorkshire hearts, hallowed by memories of school trips, and 'racial' memories, too, no doubt, of great-grandfatherly choir outings by charabanc from the industrial centres of the West Riding . . . before they changed its name, sold everyone a car and replaced homelier pleasures with gaudy package holidays. Malham is deeply recognised by many as a worthy heart of Yorkshire, its halls and farms stone-built by the yeomen who were most truly the archetypal Yorkshire-men.

A mile or so down Malhamdale I found one of the loveliest churches in the whole of the Dales, and one of the most interesting, too: St Michael's, Kirkby Malham, almost hidden behind the huge laburnum, golden with blossom in the churchyard. North of the chancel is the grave of Colonel John F. Harrison and his wife Helen – a tombstone, this, with almost a touch of 'the Taj Mahals' in its baroque cross, so that you are not surprised to learn that John spent many years abroad, presumably in India.

The Harrisons were so long separated (so the story goes) that Helen decided they should properly be still separated by water, even in death. And so, when she died in 1890, she was buried south of the stream that runs beside the churchyard. Ten years later, when John died, the ground north of the stream, selected for his grave, proved to be solid rock so man and wife had to lie together after all!

But even now a stream, barely more than a trickle, runs from a neighbouring field under an arch at the base of the tombstone and seems to perpetuate the watery separation. As I read the inscription, a vole suddenly appeared beneath the arch, then seeing me, scurried the length of the grave and disappeared into a hole at its foot. Was it a restless incarnation of one of the Harrisons, unable, after so much separation, to lie quiet beside its spouse?

Kirkby means 'village with a church'. It is a Danish usage, which places the church in pre-Conquest times (probably A.D. 800–1000), though the present building dates from about 1490. Here we see the long, low shape often met with in Craven churches, but while many, indeed most, Dales churches are beautifully sited, few have a lovelier setting than this gritstone structure with its 69-foot tower. Adam of Giggleswick gave it to the Premonstatensian abbey of West Dereham, Norfolk, and King John confirmed the gift (in one of his *less* famous charters, dated 1199).   .

Until the Reformation, its vicars were drawn from the White Canons of West Dereham. To them, the cross (of which only the base now remains) must have seemed already ancient, for it was the preaching station of their earliest predecessors, the missionaries who first called upon St Michael to repel the devils of heathendom and convert the followers of Thor and Odin to the true faith.

Like all good churches, it has a pub close by (even if the church-wardens no longer pull the pints as once they did!) In this case it is the Victoria Hotel; and to prove that even the most idyllic settings fail to breed human perfection, near the inn there are the stocks: while yet more disillusioning is the discovery that once they had a ducking stool for company.

But that, perhaps, was in the fifteenth century when the brethren of Fountains Abbey and Bolton Priory rebuilt the church. I doubt if even the stocks were still in use just a century before my visit, when Walter Morrison of Tarn House was enough of a churchman (despite his association with Charles Darwin!) to expend most of the £3,700 its restoration cost. How proud he must have been to show his distinguished visitors the signature of Oliver Cromwell (as witness to a wedding) in the church records – and how furious he would be, if he were here, to learn that those earliest records were stolen in 1972.

Yet even today he would have plenty more to show them: the niches in the pillars, for instance, empty now, which seem to wait in silent expectation for the return of tenants who quitted them, presumably, at the Reformation. They included Jesus and Mary; St Nicholas; a St Syth and St Sonday, about whom I must plead ignorance, and two more of whom even the oldest parishioner must do the same, for their names have been long forgotten. Perhaps some day they will all be rediscovered amid much rejoicing, as the eleventh-century font cover was rediscovered in 1879 . . . on a rubbish heap.

A lovely place to linger if we had less far to go. But at least notice the high box pews, in the north aisle, all different in their hand-fashioned Jacobean design. They bear the names or initials of their owners and date from 1631 to 1723.

Notice, also, the panelling in the sanctuary, placed here in 1923 as a memorial to Walter Morrison. Its heraldic meaning may be gleaned from an armorial key in the vestry, which also contains a picture (surprising, so far from the coast) of a sea-going dalesman, Captain James King, who left his birthplace to become the companion of the most famous Yorkshire sailor of them all, James Cook. And here, too, there is a portrait of Major General Lambert, the great man of Malhamdale, who fought with Cromwell and paid the price. On the vestry wall you may read (or try to) a facsimile of a grant by letters patent of the forfeited estate of 'General Lambert of Calton'. It is dated 2 April 1663 and signed by Charles II.

Now we really must leave the church, though not (however bad we may be) by the 'devil's door', opposite the main entrance. That door is blocked now – so how do the devils escape when they are driven out at baptisms? Presumably they are reduced to leaving, as must we, by the main door, taking a last look before departing at the house for which the rector must surely offer heartfelt thanks whenever he enters it. Before it became the rectory, it had been, in its time, the hall, a cotton factory and even a workhouse – what an incitement to pauperism!

North-east of Kirkby Malham is Hanlith. From here the Pennine Way leads downdale to Airton, where the Quaker meeting house dates back to the early days of the Friendly Persuasion. It was founded by one of the linen weavers who plied their trade in the village – one William Ellis, a good man and remembered because he provided coats and hoods for Friends caught out by the Malhamdale weather in its nastier moods. The houses surround the green as they have for three hundred years or so, but the old mill by the Aire, which once belonged to Bolton Priory and later housed a bottling plant, is now converted to flats.

East of Airton, a hill climbs to Calton. If it was really Cromwell's signature in that old register stolen from Kirkby Malham Church, he inscribed it while staying here with General Lambert.

What men they were, those Parliamentarians, or at least some of them! Lambert, to judge by the plaque on the gatepost of Calton Hall, was cast in the mould of his fellow-general and fellow-Yorkshireman, the great Fairfax. Born in 1619 at the hall and baptised at Kirkby Malham Church, Lambert is here praised as an 'architect of the Cromwellian Protectorate . . . a man of pleasant wit . . . great understanding'. Charles II ordered his imprisonment for life. He died in 1684, unwavering in his Republican convictions. Beneath the plaque a notice tells you that the hall is now a centre for pony-trekking.

Eastward, a narrow road wanders by way of Winterburn and Hetton to Rylstone and Wharfedale. South-west of Airton, is Otterburn – though I tried in vain to catch a glimpse of sporting otters from the single-arched bridge. And to the south lies Bell Busk, where Victorian railway trippers used to alight. Eshton, with its hall (now a school) is to the east of Bell Busk; but from Bell Busk we go south to Coniston Cold, then east to Gargrave, birthplace of one of the founders of Fountains Abbey, St Robert of Newminster Abbey, near Morpeth.

Gargrave rests neatly in the Aire Gap, grooved out by glaciers, which, as they melted, left the hillocks of boulder clay called drumlins to the south of the village. They have no doubt figured in many a skirmish, for this gap, this vulnerable break in the Pennine Chain, has been fought through by Roman, Dane, Norseman, Scot, Royalist and Lancastrian.

After so much quietude, Skipton seems almost a maelstrom of bustle, a market town where a thriving trade is done still in cattle and sheep. Its name means 'Sheeptown'; it is, if that were possible, 'more Yorkshire than Yorkshire' – a 'Gateway to the Dales' which can lay better claim to the title than most.

Its centre is its long main street at the top of which is the dignified, striking war memorial; the church and – nearby – the castle. All the principal buildings – offices, shops and on market day, the stalls, seem to line this street and on fine Saturdays the whole population of the West Riding appears to throng it. Most of them are 'passing through' – if at times their progress seems questionable – but doubtless a proportion put their cars in the enormous car park behind the High Street and take a look at the place itself.

Start with the fully roofed castle, one of the best preserved in England. Not that its career has been uneventful – far from it. . . . It stands on a cliff that rises, on the northern side, 100 feet sheer from the Haw Beck gorge. Safe enough, you might feel, from assault from the north, and protected on its other sides by a series of massive round towers. But it has fallen, in its day.

It looks impregnable enough now as you enter by the great gatehouse, with its four drum-towers, sobering even without that enigmatic word *Desormais* (Henceforth) cut in stone twice above the battlements. This was the motto of the Cliffords – for centuries Lords of the Honour of Skipton – who owned the castle during most of its history.

But it was Robert de Romille, first holder of the Honour of the grant of William the Conqueror, who built here first. Was he the original, I wonder, of Rombald the giant, whose footprints are said to be imprinted on the Cow and Calf Rocks on Ilkley or (more properly) Rombald's Moor. It is, after all, only a giant's stride from Skipton. Mighty men passed easily into legend in those credulous days, and to simple minds the sight of such a dwelling might easily have suggested the abode of a giant, or at least one whom legend enlarged to gigantic stature.

Right of the archway, the Shell Room recalls a sea-going Clifford: George, third Earl of Cumberland, one of Queen Elizabeth's admirals, and her Champion, too, who made this room a mariner's fantasy lined with coral ballast from his returning ship and ormer shells depicting Neptune, Zephyr, the sun and the moon. But of all the Cliffords, it is a woman, Admiral George's daughter, who made the strongest mark on this magnificent structure.

She was Lady Anne Clifford, born in 1590 in this same castle and her name is commemorated by Lady Anne's Steps and by a stone tablet witnessing to her work. In 1605 when Admiral (some would say pirate) George Clifford died, Lady Anne, as his closest survivor, should have inherited the castle and estates. But for some reason they passed to her uncle, and from him, to her cousin. Not until the cousin died did Lady Anne come into her own – in about 1645, when she was 55 – whereupon she set herself the task of restoring all the Clifford castles which had been damaged in the Civil War.

During that conflict the castle garrison of only 200 men, under Sir John Mallory, had withstood a three-year siege – no wonder Cromwell saw Skipton as his most formidable northern challenge. Such heroism transcended the rival causes which inspired besieged and besiegers and when at last the garrison could see no way of maintaining their stand, they were allowed by the Roundhead Colonel, Richard Thornton, to march out 'according to the Honour of a Soldier . . . with Colours flying, trumpets sounding, Drums beating . . .' to rejoin a Royalist garrison forthwith if they were fit, or, if sick or wounded, to remain at Skipton 'until it please God they shall recover and then to have Passes upon their desires to go to their home or to such of his Majesties' next Garrisons they shall make choyce of. . . .'

Furthermore, the terms of surrender, agreed on 21 December 1645, decreed 'that all the hangings and other goods given in by Inventory . . . shall be there secured . . . and not made sale of until the Lady of Pembroke be made acquainted therewith. . . .'

That Lady of Pembroke was Lady Anne and we may be sure she studied those inventories with an eye that missed no detail.

The castle's defenders had won their adversaries' respect, but that did not save the castle from being 'slighted' by Cromwell, who was determined that it should cause him no more trouble. And so, when Lady Anne returned at last to her Skipton birthplace and her inheritance in the north, only the Long Gallery was habitable. The Lady of Pembroke knew what her task must be during the remainder of her life – and it was a long one, extending to the mid-80s; she had to rebuild the family's castles – in Westmorland at Appleby, Brough, Brougham and Pendragon; in Yorkshire at Barden Tower and – one of those closest to her heart – Skipton.

Though Cromwell rumbled threats of demolition she went on with her rebuilding – as large in her resolve as she was small in stature. Only four foot ten inches, but what a character, with her smoking and her 'swounding' fits. Above all, with her love of the bleak northern country of her birth, which – as she confessed in old age – had made her earlier sojourns in the south times of anguish.

I feel sure it was Lady Anne herself who, in 1659, planted the yew tree that is still growing in Conduit Court, so named because it marks the point where the castle's supply of piped spring water was gathered into the basin from which the tree now springs. It was only a seedling, then: what would she think now of its seven-and-a-half-foot girth, or of the imposing certificates given, along with a rooted cutting, to visitors who make a £5 donation towards the maintenance of the castle. The leaves of the still-flourishing veteran cast a pleasant shade over this delightful spot – one of the oldest parts of the castle – where Anne must have loved to sit.

Many years before Anne set about restoring the castle she was born in, another, and doubtless a very different sort of woman had probably lived within its walls – though surely with none of Anne's enthusiasm for the place. She was Mary Queen of Scots and if, as tradition declares, she really spent some time here, it was as a prisoner, whose view of life from the ladies' retiring room (her probable home here) was necessarily jaundiced.

How much of the castle seen by the tragic Queen was then as we see it today? Not the Clifford motto, *Desormais*, for that was put there on Anne's instructions; nor the oak roof timbers of the watchtower, for they were added in 1659, when Cromwell's government – with memories of the siege perhaps – had forbidden flat roofs which might be used as sites for cannon. But she no doubt passed beneath the ancient Norman arch, and she too may have sat in the Conduit court, even if there was no ancient yew tree to give her shade. Her food would be prepared in the kitchen which was in use for three centuries between 1300 and 1600. But prisoner though she was, she probably saw less of the dungeons than even the casual visitor of today.

Such modern sightseers find no lack of interest in this building, so magnificently complete, in spite of Cromwell and the natural processes of decay. For the old home of the Cliffords seems to flourish in age as benignly as the yew tree itself. And the old place was surely worthy of Anne Clifford's efforts: though today the castle is devoid of contents, an inventory made on the death of the last earl lists 57 furnished apartments.

Close to the castle is the parish church, which Anne repaired after it, too, had been badly damaged in the Civil War. It is well worth visiting, if only for its splendid oak roof and beautiful sixteenth-century rood screen.

Lady Anne lives on in vivid memory, but it is good to know that modern Skipton, too, has its restorers and preservers, even if their work is on a smaller scale than hers. In 1964 one of them, George Leatt, a local cornseed merchant, bought the old corn mill on the Grassington road, not far from the church, and restored it at his own expense. There has been a water-mill here since the thirteenth century – its four wheels turned by the waters of the Eller Beck. Now two wheels have been restored, one harnessed to the millstones which again produce flour, the other providing power for all kinds of agricultural machinery – such as a hay and straw chopper, cake knutters and turnip shredders.

Here is virtually a museum of milling, but a 'functional' one, with a working blacksmith's forge, brought from Arncliffe in Littondale, and used in maintaining the waterwheels. All very much as it used to be, but how that first thirteenth-century miller would marvel at the manifestations of the electricity which the mill produces for itself, by means of a water turbine harnessed to an alternator.

No one could accuse Skipton of neglecting the past: in the Craven Museum, housed in an extension to the Town Hall, are minerals, lead-mining equipment and what is claimed to be the oldest piece of cloth in Britain – found near Rylstone in a Bronze-Age coffin 3,500 years old.

Three or four miles south-east of Skipton is the hamlet of Lothersdale. Here Charlotte Brontë found in Stonegappe (where she worked as a governess for John Benson Sidgwick) her model for 'Gateshead Hall' in *Jane Eyre*. If Charlotte's poor, overworked shade still frequents this place, I wonder what she makes of its present occupants, and how they compare with the 'perverse, riotous' Sidgwick 'cubs'. For Stonegappe is now a Youth Hostel and was, in fact, Yorkshire's very first.

The stones of Lothersdale Church would be cleanly new when she was here, for it was built in 1838, the year before she took up her unhappy appointment. I hope she enjoyed Lothersdale's pleasant peace, though doubtless she would be less impressed than we of today by the hamlet's water-wheel (in a mill) – the 'largest in England' though it may be.

Back to the main Keighley road for a look at Kildwick, with its beautiful 'Lang Kirk' of Craven. It *is* a 'lang un', an' all! – 170 feet – giving you the feeling almost that you are in the nave of a cathedral. Here are box pews, the effigy of a crusading lord of the manor, old stained glass and the pew – marked EE 1633 – once used by Edward Eltoft, Lord of the manor of Farnhill. The fine Jacobean Kildwick Hall is now a restaurant.

There are many other Craven villages worth seeing hereabouts – Elslack, Glusburn – but we are leaving 'the Dales' proper and (even more serious) heading for Lancashire if we stray too far westwards. I insist, though, that we follow the Aire as far as Keighley – with its typical West Riding blend of industry and countryside, its memories of the Brontës (for Haworth is part of Keighley) and its highly popular Keighley and Worth Valley Light Railway (much famed 'star' of the film *The Railway Children*), operated by efficient steam enthusiasts.

No chapter about the Aire could fail to mention East Riddlesden Hall, a mile and a half north-east of Keighley – for that sensitive river actually changed her course to avoid any contact with the terrible Murgatroyds who used to live there! That, at least, is the story enshrined in local tradition.

Nobody, it seems, had a good word for the Murgatroyds; they were not only fined and imprisoned by the State; the Church, too, appalled by their debauchery and profanity, declared them excommunicate. Yet perhaps they were not as bad as legend paints them, or how could they have left behind so beautiful and interesting a house?

You first view it across the 'Stagnum de Riddlesden', a fishpond, now flourishing with ducks, which helped to feed the Canons of Bolton 600 years ago, and there is a medieval tithe barn – 120 feet long with fine timbered roof and two gabled porches at each side – reckoned to be one of the best in northern England.

Is the ghost who looks out from the 'Catherine wheel' window above the two-storey porch one of the Murgatroyd clan? One of their victims, perhaps! If you are lucky (or unlucky, depending on your point of view) you may catch a glimpse of the lady; but in any case, the window is worth inspection for its own sake. It has eight lights, and is of a type believed peculiar to the West Riding. The porch it surmounts contains a doorway flanked by columns and above the circular window is a castellated roof with finials. This porch, the main body of the house to the left, and what remains of the so-called banqueting hall on the right, are very likely relics of the Murgatroyds, who built them in about 1640.

Alas for respectability – a western addition to the house, dated half a century later, and the work of more reputable owners who succeeded the

Murgatroyds, survives only as a façade, through whose pedimented, glassless windows can be seen waving tree branches. Five arched stone hutches adjoining this shell of a wing may have been mews for hawks.

Generally lawless, the Murgatroyds apparently acknowledged the claims of royalty; for heads of Charles I and Queen Henrietta Maria appear in rough relief on the battlements of a separate building of about the same date as the main house. And to prevent any doubts as to Murgatroyd allegiance there appears the motto *Vive Leroy*.

Inside the house, a National Trust property since 1934, you may see in some rooms the very same plasterwork and panelling that the Murgatroyds saw, setting off the furniture, pewter and paintings – all from the seventeenth century, of course – which the Trust placed there. A fitting place, you might feel, to take a dignified leave of Airedale.

TWO

Ribblesdale to Dentdale

A Touch of Carlislitis

Less than ten miles after leaving the splendidly Yorkshire town of Settle, the River Ribble defects to Lancashire. . . . Or so it might appear to the casual observer: I prefer to believe that, conscious of a high destiny from its birth in the Three Peaks Country, the Ribble ventures into the Red Rose realm like a missionary, bent on taking some of Yorkshire with it over the border.

To judge by what we see of Lancashire Ribblesdale, the plan is by no means a failure. Bolton-by-Bowland, Waddington and Barnoldswick have been added to Lancashire under the reorganisation of Local Government boundaries in 1974. But to the right-thinking Yorkshire-man, of course, they remain in Yorkshire and we can hardly be surprised by their merits. Witch-haunted Pendle, however, with its great, crouching hill, has always been in Lancashire and with the possible exception of Lancashire parts of the Lake District, is some of the best that Lancashire can offer. Unlike less fortunate counties, however, we in Yorkshire hardly need to poach, so they can keep Pendle – witches and all – with our blessing.

Where do I start, then, in leading you along the dale of the *Yorkshire* Ribble? It would be logical, no doubt, to begin at the river's beginning, which is unquestionably in Yorkshire, but since I plan to lead you from Ribblesdale to Dentdale and the Howgill Fells I will be guided here by the Yorkshire Dales National Park boundary and introduce you to Ribblesdale just inside it, at Long Preston; which can hardly be denied its place in this book when it has more than once been adjudged the 'Best Kept' of Dales villages.

Furthermore, this was the home of Long Preston Peggy, whose exploits are the subject of a ballad. Having walked to Preston in 1745 with the simple, feminine aim of catching a glimpse of Bonnie Prince Charlie, this obviously captivating lady found herself securing Manchester for the Jacobites! Not that she did it all on her own, you understand – she had two friends with her. . . . Then she came home to Long Preston, where the *really* important things were happening.

A few miles updale we come to a town so rich in legend that it is almost a legend in itself.

For me, the late Tot Lord epitomises Settle, as Settle itself epitomises Ribblesdale. His baptismal name was Thomas – 'Tot' was a family nickname conferred by tradition. He lived in a spacious, three-storey, fifteenth-century house in which many of his treasures were arranged, and he was the founder (or one of them) of the Pig Yard Club, a group of like-minded enthusiasts who used to meet in an Upper Settle pigyard to discuss their explorations of the caves round about.

Near that pigyard was the disused chapel which, over 40 years ago, Tot turned into a museum – the Pig Yard Club Museum, whose homely name, like Tot's own, is still honoured in speliological circles. He died years ago but he will be long remembered as an outstanding local historian. (Happily there is a move afoot to reopen Tot's museum.)

It was the Ribblesdale once inhabited by elephant and bison, woolly rhinoceros and hippo, that captured the burly Dalesman's imagination as a young man, when he first ventured into the caves in a spirit of adventure. Perhaps it was the gladiatorial sword, found in Sewell's Cave, that awoke the antiquary in him, or the remains of a chariot unearthed in fragments from Attermire Cave. Besides the skull of a Great Cave Bear (which, he would point out, was nearly twice as big as that of a grizzly of today), he prized the horns and skull of a giant ox and a reverse barb harpoon made from the antler of a red deer. These he found, like the skull, in that amazing Settle repository of prehistoric remains, Victoria Cave, discovered by a curious dog on Queen Victoria's Coronation Day in 1838. (That cave, you could say, has never lacked remarkable residents, one of the more recent being a latter-day hermit I once found living there, attired in a monkish habit of his own making.)

What Queen Victoria would have thought about this free-lancing 'monk' in *her* cave (could she have met him) I cannot imagine. On the one occasion when she visited the town, the locals took no chances of offending her sensibilities, covering up the Naked Man carving which has been displayed in Settle since 1663, when he first appeared as the sign on an inn (now a café). Anyway, he is hardly naked and his sex, I would say, is no more obvious than that of the so-called Naked Woman. Three years older than the 'man', she appears on the wall of a former inn at Langcliffe, a mile or so up-dale.

Every place, I suppose, has a personality, and few are more captivating than Settle's. This limestone market town has a charming air of eccentricity. As you approach it from the Skipton side, its stone-built houses and the many-chimneyed Falcon Hotel give an impression chiefly of solid, perhaps even dull, respectability. Interest grows as you move further into the town with its cobbled market square, from which steep and twisting lanes lead to Upper Settle, passing Preston's Folly – built as Tanner House in 1675 and, according to legend, never finished. Here in the market place is the old Shambles, whose graceful arches now set off local shopkeeper's warés. And over all rises Castleberg Crag, 300 feet high and topped by a flagpole. A product – this limestone cliff – of that great natural upheaval of long ago that produced the mid-Craven Fault.

Lime was at one time so zealously dug from the base of the crag that the good people of Settle feared the cliff might collapse and bury them! And all because, one day, a stone had tumbled down and broken a garden wall. The lime-burner was taken before the lord of the manor: that worthy forthwith empanelled a jury of 12 'wise and just men', who solemnly viewed this threat to the town and reported their findings: reassuring the townsfolk that if ever the crag fell it would fall *away* from Settle, not towards it. I hope Settle folk slept more soundly thereafter.

There is a fairy-tale quality about some of the things that have happened here. Only in Settle, surely, could a ½d. toll have been imposed on anyone rash or conceited enough to sport a new hat on market day! But not all Settle worthies were eccentrics. Dr George Birkbeck, founder of the Mechanics Institute, was born here and so was Benjamin Waugh, whose London Society for the Prevention of Cruelty to Children was a forerunner of the N.S.P.C.C. of today. A stone tablet behind the market place commemorates him. More recently Settle characters were strikingly celebrated by one of their own number – James Simpson, whose carvings of Settle personalities (including one of himself suffering the pangs of toothache) found their way into the Pig Yard Museum.

It seems all of a piece with Settle's air of amiable oddity that its name should have been linked with a strange disease whose victims evince not the slightest desire to be cured – called *Settle-Carlislitis*. This mania afflicts advanced locomaniacs whenever the Settle-to-Carlisle railway, completed in 1876, is mentioned. Its first passenger train ran on 1 May that year and on the centenary of that date, despite one of the most dismal May Days that even the old line can have seen in all its hundred years, the happy sufferers turned up at Settle in their hundreds to throng the old station, ask questions in the diminutive signal box and wait what seemed hours in a damp and draughty engine shed for a promised visit by steam locomotives which, it seemed, would never arrive.

And all to wish the Settle-Carlisle many happy returns of the day.

This £3½m. project, which at its peak engaged the energies of 6,000 men, was once compared by a Victorian Scots engineer with a giant cetacean, lying belly-down, with its nose at Settle, its tail at Carlisle!

The 'whale' measured 22 miles from its nose to the crown of its head and a further 50 miles from there to its tail end. It is still famed for its 'Long Drag' from Settle Junction to Ais Gill, where the line climbs 740 feet in little more than a thousand.

It is distinguished, also, by its straightness. It meant to get to Scotland in the fastest possible time and would brook no delays. If a hill got in the way, the Settle-Carlisle went straight through it – either by tunnelling or cutting. It has 19 viaducts and 14 tunnels. At Ais Gill it has the highest main line summit in England. In Dent it has the highest railway station in England (no longer in full use, unfortunately). Its viaducts, witness the two dozen arches of the Ribblehead, are titanic examples of Victorian architecture, built by men who clearly believed that while the impossible *might* take a little longer it had better not take *too* long.

On its birthday in 1976 it was rather more than a century old, for the first goods train ran on it in August 1875. It was the first passenger train, on May Day the following year, that added yet another significance to that all-purpose festal day, the First of May.

As the *Craven Herald* of 6 May 1876, remarked, 'Many years ago, the formation of a line . . . following the course over which Midland passengers between London and Carlisle will now be carried was declared by eminent engineering authorities to be impossible, but the impossibilities of thirty years ago are the commonplaces of today'. And yet this 'commonplace' of yesterday, built for £3½m., remember, might well be considered an impossibility today – certainly at that price!

And let no-one think this 'whale' a dinosaur. Not only is it essential to industry, but it provides one of the easiest ways to see some of the best scenery in the Dales National Park.

From Settle the A65 leads north-westwards to Ingleton, forming one side of a rough triangle with the B6255, which links it at Ingleton with another 'B' road, the 6479. It is this last we follow now – the more northerly arm of the triangle – as it takes us first of all to Langcliffe.

Langcliffe. . . . A spacious village green; children of the little school sewing in the sunshine; air filled with the cawing of churchyard rooks, and in the church porch an invitation, blessed by the vicar, to worship with the Methodists in their chapel whenever there is no service at the church.

Peace and harmony in plenty, but the scene by no means lacked activity. Clearly exempt from the Parish Council's displayed bye-laws restricting the green to invalids' or children's vehicles 'drawn by or propelled by hand', a motor-mower was being joyously driven over the grass. And across that green was a horse 'in a tew' with its tether. We tried to help and were joined by the driver of the motor-mower and an old lady from a cottage nearby (of the same type of motherly soul who, in some puzzlement, gave sandwiches and cups of tea to my hermit friend years before in Victoria Cave).

Near the green – in Langcliffe they could hardly have been far away – builders were working on a few houses. In design and material they were hardly distinguishable from the occupied ones and I could not tell whether they were new dwellings or restorations, but I envied their intended occupants. At one time they would have had Isaac Newton as an occasional neighbour during his frequent visits to the Paley family in their Tudor Hall. A road from Langcliffe leads to Malham Tarn; footpaths, too, will take you some of the way, crossing Langcliffe Scar, passing close by caverns like Victoria and Jubilee Caves and skirting the 1,536-foot Black Hill.

At Stainforth, little more than a mile to the north, water-colourists were sitting on the bank of the Ribble to paint the bridge – a graceful, single-span structure dating, some say, from the seventeenth century and sufficiently venerated to be a property of the National Trust. It has had far more to do in its time than serve as a subject for amateur painters; for quiet Stainforth was a bustling place in the eighteenth century, when packhorse men travelling between North Lancashire and the north-east stopped here for food and drink. Did the occupants of a house dated 1684 observe the construction of the bridge with lively interest? Or is it true that it was really built as early as the fourteenth century by monks of Sawley Abbey, owners of the manor after it had left the hands of Robert de Staynford and before it passed into the possession of Sir Henry Darcy?

Stainforth is no longer an 'important' stopping place on a trading highway, but in more recent years it has won a different kind of fame. William Riley, best known for his novel *Windyridge* (based on Hawksworth, Lower Airedale), wrote in another book, *A Village In Craven*, about Stainforth's cobbler-poet, Dicky Isherwood; its shopkeeper botanist, Darius Altham and about the angler-parson whose trout bait reposed in the baptismal font while christenings had to wait upon his fishing programme! And Riley was probably almost as enchanted by the water music of Stainforth and Catrigg Forces as he was by these characters. All that was 60 or 70 years ago, but doubtless then, as now, you entered the charming little church from the *western* end: though in Stainforth such a peculiarity seems hardly surprising.

The road accompanies the Ribble northwards to Horton-in-Ribblesdale at the heart of a land of giants. To the south-east is Fountains Fell (2,191 feet); north-west of that, Whernside (2,419 feet), Yorkshire's second highest summit if we could still claim Mickle Fell's 2,591 feet in Teesdale. Penyghent at 2,273 feet is lower by a hundred feet than Ingleborough to the west, whose near neighbour is Simon Fell (2,088 feet). Penyghent, Ingleborough and Whernside are Yorkshire's 'Three

Peaks', beloved of those who take pride in tramping – or cycling, or whatever – the minimum of $20\frac{3}{4}$ miles necessary to visit all three summits in one day.

The first Three Peaks Walkers – or at least, the first on record – were two teachers from Giggleswick School, Canon J.R. Wynne-Edwards and D.R. Smith. One day in 1887, weary, perhaps, of the stuffy classroom atmosphere, they set out to walk by way of Ingleborough to the Hill Inn, Chapel-le-Dale, for tea. It must say something for the Hill Inn's teas that from Chapel-le-Dale they advanced on Whernside, and having conquered that, felt they just had to tackle Penyghent, too.

Twelve hours used to be considered a reasonable time in which to 'do' the Three Peaks (and still entitles you to membership of the Three Peaks of Yorkshire Club); then two men of over 50 did it in seven and three-quarter hours and a cross-country runner completed the course in four hours twenty-seven minutes. Now there is a foot-race for Three-Peakers in the spring and one for cyclists in the autumn, though for at least five miles of the circuit they have to push or carry their machines. Not surprising, is it, that a cyclist entrant can count on losing seven or eight pounds on slopes a mountain goat might find tiring? Almost incredibly, both groups have set up records of less than three hours. For safety's sake the Three Peaks Club urges you to sign out at the Penyghent Café before embarking on the walk.

This is indeed country for the serious walkers. From Horton-in-Ribblesdale a track to the summit of Penyghent forms part of the Pennine Way, covering about 55 miles in the Dales from Gargrave in Airedale to Tan Hill (which modern heretics might claim for Durham but which none can deny is in Swaledale).

Horton's Church of St Oswald contains a brass plate brought in from the graveyard to protect it from the weather, and mysteriously inscribed: *Sacred to the memory of Richard Thornton, a short time ago schoolmaster here for the district, an honest man, fleeing from the Law, anxious to prove his innocence, and also Elizabeth, his wife. Catherine, their only daughter erected these tombstones at her own expense as a token of appreciation of the life of her dead parents. Died 29th August 1744, 57 years.*

What story lies behind these tantalising words? Of what was the honest schoolmaster accused, that he must flee from the law? Nobody seems to know.

Horton is in caver's country. Close by is the horrific Alum Pot, a huge hole in the ground 130 feet long by 40 feet wide. Into its depth of 292 feet the Alum Pot Beck hurtles in a waterfall dropping sheer for over 200 feet. Only 150 yards to the north-west is Long Churn Cave, from which a stream and passage enter Alum Pot's main shaft. Hull Pot, Penyghent Hole and Gingle Pot are other names honoured by the caving clan. It is hard to decide which are the most impressive (or terrifying, depending on your tastes). Penyghent Pot, about 500 feet deep, is one of Yorkshire's deepest, though you would hardly guess that from what you can see of it above ground. Hull Pot is nothing like so deep – a mere 60 feet (which is also its width), yet it is fully 300 feet long.

The road north-west – the 6479 – is divided from Littondale, to the east, by Fountains Fell and Penyghent. Further along, the Cam Beck follows a convoluted course.

At Ribblehead, children ate ice cream and paddled in the young Ribble, while man-made scenery in the form of 24 arches – the tallest soaring 165 feet – of the Settle-Carlisle line's viaduct, challenged the vast bulk of Whernside rising 2,419 feet behind.

Here is where some of the costliest work on the Settle-Carlisle line was done. Blea Moor Tunnel, to the north, cost an average of £45 for every one of its 2,629 yards, and the cost per mile over the line's 72-mile course was £47,500. Today the scene is almost as desolate as that of Scar House Reservoir in Nidderdale. Yet, like that wild spot, it has its share of ghosts – the navvies, some of the toughest, wildest men these islands then produced, who lived sometimes with their wives and families in the special settlement at Batty Green, or at Salt Lake City, Jericho, or some other of the colourfully named 'pioneer towns' of the day.

They drank hard, fought hard, lived, and often enough died hard. On the 6255 road (which is the connecting link in our triangle, joining Ribblehead with Ingleton), you will find the village of Chapel-le-Dale, in whose unobtrusive Church of St Leonard there is a marble wall plaque in memory of those who gave their lives – and they were many, some of them victims of a smallpox epidemic – during the building of the 'Settle-Carlisle'. Over two hundred found a resting-place in the churchyard, which had to be enlarged to accommodate them. Many of the dead, and they included not only the navvies but often their wives and children, need not have died, perhaps: the navvies' fondness for violent pastimes, like bare-knuckle fighting, and 'practical jokes', such as throwing dynamite on to the kitchen fire, doubtless played their part.

North of Chapel-le-Dale is Weathercote Cave with its 77-foot waterfall, and even Mahomet's Coffin (or at least a stone called by that name) suspended over the abyss. Further to the north-west, is the enormous Yordas Cave, 80 feet high, with a subterranean waterfall. But once we start listing these caverns it is hard to know when to stop; there is Hurtle Pot, Rowten Pot. Some, like Weathercote, may be viewed in comfort, others are beloved chiefly of those to whom discomfort is the prize of strenuous endeavour. Good luck to them!

I would simply sound a dreary note of warning and say that the difficult and dangerous ones, which include any not obviously open to the 'ordinary' tourist, should be avoided by all but the experts or those under expert supervision and properly equipped. White Scar Cave, further along the road to Ingleton, is one of the caverns with spectacular stalactites and stalagmites, which can be explored in comfort and safety. It penetrates the side of Ingleborough for half a mile.

It is a thought worth pondering, that but for the tourists who came here via the railway from about the mid-nineteenth century, the watery attractions of the district might have remained long unsuspected. However, once the waterfalls and gorges in the Twiss and Doe valleys were discovered, the local inhabitants, allied by the railway company, were quick to make them available to the visiting public. Ingleton's three-mile 'Falls Walk' is still justly famous for its enchanting tree and river scenery.

We set out on the last arm of our Ribblesdale triangle now, making for Settle by way of the A65 which soon brings us to Clapham near the junction of the B6480 from High Bentham. Another splendid cave here – the most famous in the north, says its publicists – which extends for a third of a mile beneath Ingleborough. It is certainly among the most impressive, with its huge stalactite chambers lit by electricity. You reach it through the grounds of Ingleborough Hall, following the stream and then walking along the lakeside.

Above the cave is another 'roofless cave', hardly another Gordale Scar, but perhaps having a similar history. The path which ends at Ingleborough's 2,373-foot summit leads also to Gaping Ghyll, which in August the public may descend with the aid of the Craven Pothole Club.

If you decide to climb Ingleborough, watch out for Dame Alice Ketyll, the Witch of Clapham! She lived in a cottage at the foot of Trow Gill and her foster-son, John de Clapham, lived at Clapdale Hall (or castle, as it was once called). Despite his rather superior address, John was not thriving and so Alice asked aid from the devil.

As always, that gentleman was agreeable, but as always, there were conditions: between compline and curfew Alice had to sweep the dust of Clapham Bridge towards the castle, thus ensuring that all the wealth of Clapham would go the same way . . . *provided* she fulfilled another condition. She had to place nine newly-killed red cocks around her on the bridge and call for Robyn Artisson, whom Satan had appointed to be her familiar spirit and to fulfil her every wish. Should she fail once to produce the cocks, her soul was forfeit.

No doubt you can guess what happened. Well, could *you* guarantee to find nine red cocks every night? Neither could Alice. So she lost that bargain, written in fiery letters and signed in her own blood, and became a witch and the devil's bond servant. According to all the rules, her soul should have been in the infernal regions these many years now, but watch out – you never know with witches!

A pleasanter encounter might once have been enjoyed with Reginald Farrer, who lived at Ingleborough Hall and became known as the 'Father of English Rock Gardening'. His rockery, rich in plants, brought home from sometimes perilous globe-trotting, was known throughout the world. On returning to the hall, it is said, his first call was always the potting shed where he would make his latest finds comfortable even before renewing acquaintance with his family. Sometimes he would even sleep amongst the plants. He died in 1920 aged no more than 40, while plant-hunting in Burma, but he has his memorials. Not only his books, such as *The Rainbow Bridge* and *The Garden of Asia*, but a stone column with an inscription declaring, *He loved God's works and blessed the world by many glorious flowers named after him.* And those flowers, with names like *Gentiana farreri* or *Lilium farreri*, are undoubtedly his best memorial of all.

What names there are for the villages hereabouts – Mewith Head, Keasden, Eldroth, Lawkland, Wham – they sound like places in a story by Tolkien.

Reached by way of a detour from the A65, Austwick was *en fête* on the last summer day I spent there. The drone of model aircraft competed with the noise of a tractor in the next field for this was the time of the hay harvest. There was a puppy race, pony rides, a cave rescue ambulance from Clapham on show; and at half an hour before midnight a torchlight procession in which, perhaps, the ghosts of Vikings joined.

From Austwick a footpath leads northwards for a mile to one of those sights which frequently enough remind us that we are in the Dales – and could hardly be anywhere else. I refer to another of those remarkable manifestations of glacial action, the Norber Boulders. Here the Ice Age has literally turned nature upside down by depositing glacier-borne rocks of the Ordovician series on top of the later carboniferous limestone – with striking results. For the surrounding limestone has in many cases been eroded, leaving the boulders (or erratics, as geologists like to call them) on platforms or pedestals, up to two feet in height, formed of the remaining limestone which their protecting bulk has saved from erosion.

Austwick leads to the hamlet of Wharfe, and the road on which this handful of houses stands then divides, one arm joining the main Settle-to-Horton road, the other passing through Little Stainforth and Stackhouse before landing up near Giggleswick on the road from Settle to Ingleton.

Giggleswick. . . . George Fox, the founder of the Society of Friends, found few friends there, it seems (and not much to laugh at, either), when in 1665, he was held prisoner at the village inn. He was probably still feeling injured after his experiences at Bentham and at Lancaster, where he was imprisoned in the castle for following his beliefs. With a frankness worthy even of a Yorkshireman, he told the castle officer, before leaving Lancaster for Bentham, that he had 'received neither christianity, civility nor humanity, from them.'

Though he was hardly strong enough to ride 'they hurried me away . . . to Bentham'. Things were little better there, for 'the wicked jailer, one Hunter a young fellow, would come behind, and give the horse a lash with his whip, and make him skip, and leap: so that I, being weak had difficulty to sit him; and then he would come and look me in the face and say, "How do you, Mr Fox?" I told him "it was not civil in him to do so". The Lord cut him off soon after'. Poor, wicked Mr Hunter!

Nobody, it seemed, had warned the folk at Giggleswick of the dangers of such behaviour, for the prophet of the Inner Light found little more civility at Giggleswick, where, arriving late at night, his escort 'raised the constables with their clog-shoes, who sat drinking all the night in the room with me, so that I could not get much rest'. It can have been little consolation to Fox that the inn closely adjoined the church (the 'steeple house', as he might have called it – though it has no steeple), for as was often the case, the hostelry was owned by the church which had an exit from the churchyard directly into the inn. A splendid building, Giggleswick church, dating largely from the fifteenth century. As a rather odd neighbour for its knightly effigies, it has a monument to Dr Birkbeck, whom we met at Settle.

To Giggleswick's famous school came Sir Matthew Smith, the Halifax-born painter of glowing nudes, flowers and landscapes. He had perhaps left Giggleswick for Manchester School of Art when the first moves were made to give Giggleswick, and Ribblesdale itself, one of its best-known landmarks – the copper dome on Giggleswick School's chapel. And here, once again, we meet Walter Morrison, of Malham Tarn House . . . and Queen Victoria.

The Queen Empress, whose eyes had to be protected from the Settle's poor, harmless Naked Man, and whose name was bestowed on a limestone cave hereabouts, seems to figure largely in the history of the area. It was to mark her Diamond Jubilee that Morrison erected a chapel for the ancient 'Gramer Schole' whose original charter was granted by Edward VI in 1553. The chapel's copper dome roof (now blending with the green of the landscape) was Morrison's idea – he seems to have felt there was a shortage of domes in England: his, too, the suggestion of a stained glass window representing five school worthies, including the headmaster, the Revd. George Style, and the Revd. James Carr, who founded the school in a cottage in 1512.

For centuries Giggleswick's new-boys must have been told about the town's Ebbing and Flowing Well at the foot of Buckshaw Brow. 'It niver does owt when Ah'm lookin' at it', complained a local, but I am assured that other visitors have been more favoured.

Giggleswick School, now one of the North's best-known public schools, has been a stern establishment at some periods of its long history. In 1592 the boys began work at 6.30 a.m. and slogged away till five (with a much-needed break from eleven to one), the seniors studying under a master who was ordered to address them only in Greek, Latin or Hebrew. But there were livelier times when, for instance, the school held its annual March 'cock-feight', with school governors, as well as villagers, cheering on their fancies. Another yearly event was Potation Day, when the boys consumed quantities of bread and figs – with the aid, surely necessary, of school beer!

I wonder if the school's life was more closely interwoven, in those days, with the life of the village. At any rate, I doubt if the head boys nowadays earn a guinea by reciting a Latin ode at weddings (and I wonder whether, in most cases, the happy pair understood much more of the verse than they would today).

At the top of Ribblesdale, Whernside signals the paradoxical fact that although we may pass beneath the shadow of its 2,419 feet to enter the 'new county' of Cumbria, we remain in the Yorkshire Dales National Park. Which is sure to be seen by the die-hard Yorkshire traditionalist, according to his mood, as either a slight consolation or an aggravated irritation!

The planners and revisers, it would seem, can abide anything better than variety: and since Yorkshire, as it used to be, abounded in that particular spice, they must erase the Ridings, detach us from Cleveland in the North and the eastern wolds and boil down what remains, skimming from the surface of the resulting soup whatever might add piquancy. Alas, they'll never make good cooks.

They probably felt that in the case of Dentdale and Garsdale they had a double reason for spoiling the broth (to conclude my culinary metaphor). Dentdale, it could be said, has a westerly affinity with the Lake District towards which it leads. Furthermore, it stuck out oddly from the old Yorkshire boundary (though anything less deserving to be called a sore thumb it would be difficult to imagine). However, tidiness and homogeneity seem to have proved overwhelmingly desirable, because this delectable 'peninsula' – beautiful, remote and full of history and tradition – is now part of 'Cumbria'.

Between Whernside and Dentdale lies Deepdale on the road from Thornton-in-Lonsdale (near Ingleton), which affords one of the most impressive approaches to a countryside of superb mountain scenery and waterfalls.

Dent Town, once capital of the ancient kingdom of Dent, is now a village of cobbled streets with a church, at first sight seeming almost as big as the village itself. The chancel floor is of marble – Dent marble – with a border of limestone-marble from Barrow. And the reason for that is that Dent was once famous for its black marble industry.

Proud housewives as far away as Liverpool or London would bask in the reflected glow of their fireplaces of Dent marble, while in grander settings it made highly impressive ornamental floors. But that was before Italian marble began to be imported, a sad blow, because it came at just about the same time – 1876 – as the Settle-Carlisle line which gave Dent that highest main line railway station in England. Before that, the marble had been taken by packhorse for onward transmission by means of the Leeds-Liverpool Canal.

Dent Station is happily once more in limited use, for in recent years the 'Dales Rail' service has reopened this and other old stations on the Settle-Carlisle line as summer halts for the benefit of visitors to the National Park who either have no transport of their own or prefer to 'park and ride' to the great relief of the Dales roads – which will remain so much the less crowded for the greatly appreciated service.

And it is not only the visitors who benefit: farmers and their wives in the remote Dales areas have now a choice of visiting Bradford or Leeds or Carlisle by this relaxing mode of transport for a day's shopping. How pleasant to see 'progress' so agreeably put into reverse for once!

Adam Sedgwick would have been delighted. He was Dentdale's most noteworthy son, who died three years before regular passenger services began on the line, so he never had the pleasure of seeing his native dale from that unique 700-foot vantage point.

He would surely have loved to travel home that way from Cambridge, where he was a highly distinguished Professor of Geology, for he never lost his love of the dale. Neither has it forgotten him, as a tablet in the church bears witness, recording that he constantly re-visited 'his beloved birth-dale . . . with increasing affection'. Still more striking and appropriate is the huge slab of Shap granite outside the churchyard which bears his name and serves also as a drinking fountain.

Sedgwick loved to appear the countryman he always remained at heart. Once, taking him for a yokel, the poet William Howitt (author of *Rural Life in England*) condescended to chat and then doled out a parting gift of half-a-crown – for which Sedgwick expressed his thanks when, to Howitt's astonishment, they met at a high-powered meeting in London.

Dent is best known of all for its history of 'terrible' (or remarkable) knitters. Knitting was at one time a highly organised local industry in the Dales and not just in Dentdale, though Dent became particularly famous for 'Terrible Knitters' as a result of the use of that term by the poet Southey in a book of local tales.

Sedgwick himself wrote much about life in bygone Dent Town, where the houses had galleries, which, though they may have 'almost shut out the sight of the sky from those who travelled on the pavement . . . formed a highway of communication to a dense and industrious rural population which lived in flats or single floors'. We rarely associate flat dwellers with eighteenth-century Dales life.

Sedgwick could hardly have failed to write about Dent's knitters, and he records 'little groups of family parties, who assembled together in rotation round one blazing fire, during the winter evenings'. They called it 'gangin' a sittin'' and the object of it was, of course, to knit!

By the flickering light of a peat or log fire they would perform with amazing speed to the accompaniment, when possible, of a spell-binding reading, by some youngster, perhaps, who could offer a chapter of *Robinson Crusoe* or *Pilgrim's Progress*.

Men, women and children knitted. At special schools small children were required to produce prodigious quantities of knitting and some of them, unable to stand it, ran away to other parts of the Dales, where, it is good to know, they found people more sympathetic with the needs of childhood. Perhaps one of the most profitable parts of the trade was held by the 'stockingers' who collected the caps, stockings and so on, produced by the knitting families, for dispatch to London.

Dentdale follows the course of the River Dee from Stone House, by way of Lea Yeat, Dent and Gawthrop to Sedbergh, with Rise Hill (1,825 feet) on the northern side of the valley challenging Whernside's loftier stature on the south. There is a far greener, more pastoral look about Dentdale. There are more hedges than walls, at least in the lower fields and more farms – many whitewashed and with porches, Yes, undoubtedly it has a 'Lakes look'.

Sedbergh, with its small but ancient market, is the metropolis of this lovely area. All the roads and the rivers Clough and Dee and Rawthey seem to be travelling there in a leisurely but purposeful fashion. So we, too, will stop at Sedbergh for a while before venturing to explore the Howgill Fells, rising smooth and slaty, over 2,000 feet to the north of the town, so obviously different, in their green-rounded contours, from the other hills and mountains of the Dales.

Yes, let me admit it – Sedbergh, too, *has* more the look of a Lakeland town than it has of a Dales village. And there are those who feel it quite fair that it should be handed over to Cumbria, whilst remaining the largest town in the Dales National Park; because, they say, it has been in Yorkshire only since the twelfth century. What! A mere eight centuries or so? How lucky that we were able to give it back before anyone noticed and accused us of poaching. . . .

Sedbergh, like Dent, had its knitters but in the late eighteenth century they switched to the cotton trade. Weavers' Yard reminds us of them still, though there can be few weavers in Sedbergh today. It is better known now for its public school than for its industry – and for its memories of George Fox.

In Sedbergh's parish church of St Andrew there is preserved a fragment of the yew tree under which Fox preached in Sedbergh churchyard in 1652, which rather goes to show how much Anglican vicars have mellowed in their attitude towards the Quakers' founder since the time when early Friends were fined for not going to church.

Briggflatts Meeting House is virtually a Quaker shrine – if the Friends will forgive me for using the word. Like most such buildings it has a beautiful simplicity – stone-built, slate-roofed, with white walls and an arched porch looking out on to a delightfully colourful garden. It dates from 1675, and when the ground on which it stands was bought in the previous year, Quaker meetings were still against the law. But the Friends lacked neither faith nor resources. Everyone gave what he had towards the building, whether he could best afford oak from his land or only the labour of his hands. Even so, the Friends had little to keep them warm but a hearth fire at the west end and their own fervour; for the building lacked a ceiling, and during the cold weather two of the members had the job of sealing out the rain and snow with moss stuffed between the slates.

Follow the A683 from Sedbergh along the course of the River Rawthey, and near Bluecaster and Haygarth, just inside the old border with Westmorland, you will see Cautley Spout careering 800 feet in a series of falls down the side of the Calf (2,219 feet).

The approach to the Spout is signalled by the Cross Keys Inn (Temperance) which announces its harmless character with a sign depicting a bottle of ginger beer and a cup of tea. Built about 1600, but altered in later centuries, it belongs to the National Trust which acquired it in 1949. It had been left to the Trust along with 17 acres, by Mrs E.A. Bunney, in memory of her sister.

The sign to the Spout admonishes, 'Take only photographs. Leave only footprints'. Another sign – warning of sheep-worrying – had grim support, when I last climbed towards the falls, in the form of a dead sheep, a sad fact in such a lovely setting, ignored by its flock-mates and by the ponies which leapt and ran when you approached them – almost like the foam-flecked water of the Spout itself.

Only a few miles, now, to the National Park boundary, but since we are already in Cumbria, we may as well trespass a little further by following the road till it joins the Kendal road and then accompanying it as far as Kirkby Stephen. From here you may cross Mallerstang Common with the River Eden, passing what remains of Lammerside and Pendragon Castles to rejoin the Hawes-Garsdale Road just inside Wensleydale at the Moorcock Inn.

Garsdale cuts a deep furrow between Baugh Fell and Rise Hill. The Settle-Carlisle line crosses the road and we see Garsdale Station a little way before a road leads off, right, to Grisedale – *The Dale that Died* Barry Cockcroft called it in his book based on a film he made for Yorkshire Television.

Grisedale is a secret place, hidden among great fells like that long ago given the name *Wild Boar*, which rises 2,324 feet to block Grisedale's northern end. You don't come upon Grisedale too easily: it tries to hide itself behind No Through Road signs and rather deviously leads you back to the main Sedbergh road; and before you enter Grisedale itself, you have to open a gate crossing the road.

'Grisedale 2', said the main road sign, and the dale itself is no longer than that, and only half a mile wide, hedged in by the great fells. A ghostly place this, with ruined farms and a beck that seems to chatter to itself for sheer loneliness.

King Arthur himself may have walked here: Pendragon Castle in Mallerstang is not far away and there were those who said that his father was Uther Pendragon. (How reasonable, after all, if Arthur should prove to be a Yorkshireman with such a splendidly Yorkshire Christian name! Anyway, we all know he's asleep beneath Richmond Castle waiting till England needs him again. A heavy sleeper, did you say?)

The Vikings named Grisedale; for *gris* is a Norse word for pig, and this dale sealed by Wild Boar Fell is still called Pig Valley by older dalesmen. They say, too, that when the wild boar had been hunted almost to extinction by Brigante, Roman and Dane, the last surviving pack found sanctuary for a time in the Grisedale wilds.

But Pig Valley has produced more than pigs in its time. Vivid characters like Richard Atkinson, the rip-roaring, fiddle-playing game-keeper-turned-evangelist, founder of 'Dick Atkinson's Disciples', who declined an invitation to preach in London so that he might concentrate his efforts in the Dales – or did he feel perhaps that Londoners were beyond redemption? More probably, his decision reflected the isolation of Grisedale in the 1880s – and a half-conscious belief, maybe, that here was the only world that really mattered.

I have no space to recount the hard times which led to Grisedale's decline and apparent death in recent decades, or the hopes of rebirth kindled when a former coalminer named Joe Gibson and his wife began farming here alone. But follow the sign to Grisedale – at least, even now, you won't complain of the crowds.

And having returned to the main highway, go with the tumbling River Clough with its many bridges as it runs westward to join the River

1 Thwaite, in Swaledale, birthplace of the naturalist brothers Richard and Cherry Kearton

2 Dales Farm, Capon Hall, near Malham Tarn, the largest natural lake in the West Riding

3 Rocks at Malham Cove

4 Brant Fell, north-east of Sedbergh

5 The Sun Inn at Dent Town, once the capital of an ancient kingdom

6 Ingleborough, one of the famed three peaks, from the River Doe

7 *opposite:* The Ribble at Stainforth Bridge, beloved of water-colourists

8 Arncliffe – Cowside Beck and St. Oswald's Church, containing memories of Dalesmen who fought at Flodden Field

Rawthey about a mile above Sedbergh. Midway, there is the only community in Garsdale – a little group of buildings comprising houses, church, chapel and school – called simply The Street.

THREE

Valley of the Wharfe
'Classic' of the Dales

Wharfedale might be called the *classic* dale. It has everything a dale should have, from the Wharfe's rising amid the wastes of Langstrothdale Chase, where Norman lords once killed their deer, to its union with the Ouse near Cawood – wildly beautiful mountain scenery, storied villages, mysterious ghylls and caverns, old inns, some of which might have grown out of the very limestone. And in its offspring, Littondale, it has one of the most delectable of the 'little dales'.

Wharfedale has its ruined castles, too, or what remains of them, and a priory which must be one of the best loved and most visited spots in Yorkshire.

But where does Wharfedale begin? Whoever delineated the boundaries of the Yorkshire Dales National Park and drew the red dotted line a mile or so south of Beamsley with its circular almshouse, founded in 1593, might disregard what others call the Lower Dale. If so, they leave out too much for my taste.

Undoubtedly Wharfedale comes into its own above Ilkley, but between Cawood and Otley there is a stretch of rich riverside country with a wealth of interest and variety – castles, great houses, the scene of a murderous battle, towns once known to the Romans – 'everything', you might say, except the more austere beauty of the upper reaches of the dale, to which these gentle miles serve as a most worthy curtain-raiser.

And so I start *my* Wharfedale at Cawood, where for a time lived the Mitred Peacock, as Mother Shipton called Wolsey, because his splendour then was hardly surpassed by that of the king himself.

Of all the Knaresborough-born seer's prophecies, one of the best authenticated may well be that in which she declared that Wolsey would see, but never be enthroned at, York. Nor was he – and that was fortunate for her, because he had retorted to her prophecy that when he was, his first task would be to burn her as a witch. He got as far as Cawood, for long the seat of Archbishops of York, and though from there he could see the towers of York Castle, eight miles away, he approached no nearer; for at Cawood he was arrested by the Earl of Northumberland and taken south to face trial for high treason. He died on the way, at Leicester.

Today the gatehouse of Cawood Castle, ornately fashioned from the creamy local limestone, is all that remains of the splendour once enjoyed here by Archbishops of York. Though now part of a private house, the gatehouse has still the beautiful oriel windows that must have won the admiration of the guests of Archbishop George Neville, brother of Warwick the Kingmaker, when he threw a party here which has entered into legend. Two thousand cooks were needed to deal with a menu that included 1,000 sheep, 2,000 geese, 400 swans, 500 stags, bucks and does and 104 oxen. Not forgetting 1,000 capons, 2,000 chickens, 4,000 pigeons, plus the same number of mallard and teal; 500 partridges, 400 woodcock, as many plover and 100 curlews. To make sure no corners went unfilled there were venison pasties – 1,500 hot and 4,000 cold; and custards (always, apparently, a popular Yorkshire dish), 2,000 hot and 3,000 cold.

The white church beside the river had already been here for centuries when Wolsey arrived. They say he was the original of Humpty Dumpty and there is a legend – if it is no more – that after his 'great fall' he was hidden for a time from the 'King's men' in the cellar of the Ferry Inn.

A little to the north, the Wharfe marries the Ouse, the river which bore the Vikings to York; but I saw no sea raiders as I looked downstream from the iron bridge: there was hardly room for them for the three water-skiers being towed by a motor-boat at a speed the ancient mariners would have found hard to credit.

Those Danes, I would guess, left their memorial in the name of one village hereabouts – Ulleskelf – while its neighbour Ryther perpetuates the name of the family whose fine medieval monuments adorn the south aisle of the village church. Across the river at Bolton Percy is Nun Appleton Hall, where Cromwell's greatest general, Thomas Fairfax, plotted to restore a Stuart to the English throne.

Great warriors though the Vikings were, they saw no battle to match that fought just a few miles west of here. It bears the name of a sleepy village – and the bloodiest reputation of any battle fought in England. Did 40,000 men really die in combat at Towton Field on Palm Sunday, 1461? Did the little River Cock run red with their blood on its way to the Wharfe?

It happened during the Wars of the Roses, which nowadays first suggest, to most people, nothing more sanguinary than a Lancashire-Yorkshire cricket duel. But the picking of roses as badges probably happened only in Shakespeare's imagination, and the flowers, though emblems of the Houses of York and of Lancaster, were not yet symbols of our sister counties. Even so, there was a time, or so they say, when little wild roses, white with a red spot suggesting a drop of blood, grew here . . . until they were rendered extinct by souvenir gatherers.

Today they are as hard to find, I suppose, as the bones and weapons which used to be turned up occasionally by the plough near the tiny Lead Church, which stands mysteriously in the middle of a field. Built as early perhaps as the twelfth century, it was already there when the shouts of battle and the clash of steel made mockery of its gentle message, for there have been many battles more 'Christian' than Towton, in which no prisoners were taken, no quarter given – by mutual agreement.

But it was no fair contest, for nature – or God, as the Yorkists must have thought – joined in on their side, hurling a violent snowstorm full in the Lancastrians' faces, impeding their vision and shortening the flight of their arrows.

The Yorkists advanced with the snowflakes, cutting down the demoralised foe. At first the Lancastrians retreated, still fighting; then, all hope gone, they ran. But encumbered by armour, they stumbled and those who fell into the Cock were run over by their comrades.

The story is quickly told, but the fighting lasted, say the chroniclers, for ten hours. 'Exaggeration', snort the historians of today, 'like the numbers of the dead'. But the modern historians were not there. Certainly the sons of many of Yorkshire's great families and their followers were killed; because, paradoxically, most of the Yorkshire aristocracy supported the Lancastrian cause.

The shouts of battle on that long and bloody day were heard at Hazlewood Castle nearly two miles away – though the castle was not then as it appears today; it had not yet been 'Georgianised' by Sir Walter Vavasour. Perhaps the eighteenth-century Sir Walter, whose family occupied the castle for 800 years, felt it was in danger of being eclipsed by the house which Robert Benson began building near the village of Bramham in 1698.

Bramham Park is still occupied today by descendants of that Robert Benson whom Horace Walpole called 'a person of no extraction'. More impressed, perhaps, Queen Anne created him the first Lord Bingley in 1713, after he had already distinguished himself by becoming Lord Mayor of York and an M.P., like his father, as well as a Commissioner of the Exchequer.

Bramham Park is notable if not unique in Britain for its Queen Anne gardens landscaped in the French manner, with beech hedges, tree-lined walks and ornamental cascades, and for its furniture and paintings.

Surely the Dales contain everything, though they might easily have lost Bramham Park. A fire proved so disastrous in the nineteenth century that the house had to be restored between 1906 and 1914 (the depleted family finances would not run to it until then) and before that the family had to find other lodgings for many years. Then in 1962 the furious February gales uprooted hundreds of the garden's trees. A tragedy to tree-lovers, but the fact that Bramham Park could apparently spare them so easily shows how many must have been there to start with.

Hazlewood Castle is home to a Roman Catholic community, who cherish the skulls of two recusants executed at York. The Vavasours, who lived here for so long, would certainly approve. Even in Elizabeth I's reign, mass continued to be said, with royal permission, in the chapel at Hazlewood.

Tadcaster is the eastern point of a triangle formed with Wetherby and Bramham Park. A bustling town, apparently all pubs and breweries, its assertive chimneys soar over the surprised countryside. Even a museum, The Ark, located in a fifteenth-century house, is dedicated to beer and brewing and is owned by John Smith's, one of the breweries which employ so many of the townsfolk.

Tadcaster has very much the air of a country town. A by-pass has eased traffic between Leeds and York over a five-arched bridge, which, though widened since the seventeenth century, when it was built, still seemed too narrow. From that bridge you see a white limestone church, always a pleasing surprise, to my eyes at least, and a reminder that about ten miles away, built from the same sort of stone, is York Minster. The stone, in fact, was dug here from quarries owned by the Vavasours of Hazlewood – one reason, perhaps, why they enjoyed royal favour? Today, Tadcaster's Church of St Mary looks so settled in its riverside niche that you would never suspect it had been here little more than a century. Yet so it has. On its original site it was in constant danger of flooding, so in 1877 it was painstakingly dismantled to be reconstructed on a safer site.

Follow the Wharfe, by way of Newton Kyme, with its Hall and avenues of limes planted by Admiral Robert Fairfax, of the great Parliamentarian family. Pass Clifford with its holy well, and Boston Spa, once famed for its chalybeate water, and you will eventually come to Wetherby, where the Roman Emperor Severus is said to have run the first horse race in England, and where you may still see strings of race horses at exercise. For Wetherby, beloved of the racing fraternity, has its own racecourse. Nowhere is the feel of the Turf more noticeable than in the Swan and Talbot Inn, where any small, wiry-looking man seems certain to be a jockey and where photo-finish pictures adorn the roof beams, as well as photographs of bygone winners, a saddle and the racing colours and cap of some champion rider of long ago.

Leave the A1 (once the Great North Road) at Wetherby's thunderously busy roundabout and travel by the A58 to Collingham and thence by a still quieter and pleasanter road towards Harewood.

South-west of Collingham is Bardsey, which claims to have not only the oldest inn in England, the Bingley Arms, but to be the birthplace of one of England's great playwrights, William Congreve. Just how big (or how small) a part was played in William's life by his birthplace is hard to say. He could have spent very little time in the village where he was born (in the house of Sir John Lewis, his mother's great-uncle) for quite soon he left Bardsey to live in Ireland, where his father was serving as an army officer. From Ireland he went to London. He met Dryden, showing him his comedy *The Old Bachelor*, and before he was 23 had seen it successfully staged at the Theatre Royal, Drury Lane.

From then, as Yorkshiremen like to say, 'he never looked back'. . . . I wonder if he ever looked back to Bardsey, or even thought about it. And what, for that matter, did Bardsey think about having produced the man who was to be reckoned greatest of the Restoration dramatists? Probably nothing at the time, though today William is remembered at least in a street name.

What, I wonder, is so special about East Keswick that four little roads leave the road to Harewood to journey to this mid-Wharfedale village whose name suggests the Lake District; while yet another road brings you here out of a maze-like pattern threading through quiet fields dotted with Bardsey, Wike, Scarcroft, Slaid Hill. . . .

Time was when there was good reason to take any road that offered to East Keswick. Owen Bowen lived there in his old age, after leaving Collingham. He was still painting in his nineties – having made mid-Wharfedale his own in oils as surely as Fred Lawson captured Wensleydale in water-colour. The sprightliest of octogenarians, Bowen talked to me once about the revered Edmund Bogg, whose Yorkshire books he helped to illustrate; and about his own tiny painting in the Queen's doll's house of Goldsborough Hall, near Knaresborough, where once the Princess Royal lived.

And so to Harewood, and memories of two of the legendary figures who help to convince most Yorkshiremen that there really must be something special about the country that produced them. I refer to Horbury-born John Carr, who designed Harewood House itself, and to Thomas Chippendale, born not far away at Otley who made a great deal of the furniture.

The somewhat mysterious Chippendale we shall meet at Otley. So what of Carr? There is little mystery, I think, about him. A Vanbrugh he was *not* – a worker he certainly was. Immensely prolific, except of children, he lived a life punctuated by work on one great house after another – Heath Hall, Wakefield (which he extended), Constable

Burton Hall near Bedale, the stables at Castle Howard, Temple Newsam, Boynton Hall. . . . If he was not building such he was advising their owners on alterations, or adding a library, or rebuilding something else in the Palladian or occasionally the Gothic or neo-classic styles. And he still found time to be Lord Mayor of York twice, a county surveyor of bridges, a West Riding magistrate and a popular singer at social events!

In his retirement he would take his beloved nieces, who perhaps replaced the children that had been denied him, on tours to see his works. What a mellow character he must have been, what an advertisement for a life of honest industry and endeavour! Yet he had been so poor in his youth that he had to stay in bed while his only trousers were being mended.

A designer of bridges, churches, hospitals and a grand-stand for York race-course, he is said to have changed the face of much of the eighteenth-century northern countryside, and he surely transformed the village of Harewood.

John Carr may have been, and probably was, a good-natured man. He was also undeniably a shrewd one – two good reasons why he apparently made no touchy protest when Robert Adam, who was making sketches for the restoration of Harewood Church at the time, 'tickled up' Carr's plan as his brother James put it, 'to dazzle the eyes of the squire', adding statues and other embellishments, as well as more drastic alterations, so that in some respects the house is a compromise between the ideas of Carr and Adam.

Carr designed Harewood House for Edwin Lascelles in 1759, when he was about 36, and the commission was seminal for him in that he came in contact there with the work of the Adam brothers. Having designed the house, he re-designed the village outside its gates. One *supposes* the villagers of the time approved of the transformation. I have never found an account of the original village (variously called Heraward, Whorewood or Harwood during its long history), but it could hardly have much resembled the Harewood which finally emerged from Carr's design.

As an example of Corinthian design, Harewood House is undeniably splendid, and indeed its setting demands that it should be so. Capability Brown, who designed the park of about 1,800 acres, rarely had more promising material. On the skyline rises Alms Cliff Crag, no Everest, even if real mountaineers do train on its rocky surfaces of millstone grit 600 feet above sea-level, but a striking sight nevertheless with its own touching story of a lovelorn girl whose crinoline foiled her attempt to commit suicide by jumping from the top. In what must have been the first parachute descent in history – if an unintentional one – she suffered no more than a sprained ankle and was understandably furious.

But Edwin Lascelles had not only his personal 'mountain' in sight of his mansion, but an actual castle, built in the fourteenth century on the site of an earlier one raised soon after the Conquest. Gaunt upon its ridge, this authentic relic of medievalism must have been a priceless acquisition in that age which so loved the 'Gothic' that a mere imitation ruin was so much better than nothing. Also within the grounds, Harewood Church, with its alabaster tombs, dates from the reign of Edward III. It replaced a church built when the castle itself was founded.

Today the castle shell is no longer safe enough for visitors to enter. If they could, they would see over the main entrance the crest of Sir William Aldburgh who built it in 1367 on rather more ornamental lines than had been customary with the Normans. With the crest is the family motto *What shall be, shall*.

Besides the Aldburgh arms there appears here the badge of John Balliol, King of Scotland. Surprising, perhaps, until you know that Sir William was an officer in Balliol's court. Indeed, this ruined castle, to be seen from the road from Otley to Wetherby, was once a royal refuge, for John Balliol fled to this place when he lost his crown.

And still I have not described the house's contents – a hopeless task in a paragraph or two. One name inevitably leads all the rest – that of Robert Adam, since it was he who orchestrated the brilliance of Chippendale, whose bills still exist at the house; the talents of the decorative painters Angelica Kauffmann and her husband Antonio Zucchi and Biagio Rebecca and the stuccoists' skill of Joseph Rose, of York, and William Collins.

Both house and gardens are open to the public, who prize them as peculiarly Yorkshire possessions – especially since the house was formerly the home of the Princess Royal, cherished as Yorkshire's 'own' member of the Royal Family. Her son, the Earl of Harewood, lives there today, when it is doubtless more popular than ever with the public due to such attractions as the exotic bird garden and a special house where equally exotic butterflies and other insects may be seen live at various stages of their life cycle. The present earl, a descendant of that Edwin Lascelles who commissioned John Carr to build the house, survived the war despite having his death warrant signed by Hitler when he was a prisoner in Colditz Castle.

Having joined the A61 opposite the main gates to Harewood House, the A659 skirts Harewood Park for a time before regaining its independence near Harewood Bridge and resuming its quiet way to Arthington, where Nunnery Farm, now a private house, takes its name from a Cluniac retreat founded hereabouts by Peter de Arthington in about 1150. The nunnery was dissolved in 1540 and from its remains the present house was built in about 1585.

It is unmistakably recognised from the road as 'the house with all the windows', though until recent years the windows were by no means all they seemed. At first sight there were three rows of them, extending almost the full length of the 22-yard south front of the house. But most of the top row were windows that admitted no light, for their 'panes' were slate with 'bars' of white paint. They had been so blinded since their owner first employed that stratagem to beat the window tax. Was that first owner Thomas Briggs, who incorporated in his dwelling a stone spiral stairway that is said to have come from the old nunnery? A fine example of West Riding vernacular architecture, the house has long been admired for its plaster ceilings with their vine and acorn motifs. And how truly 'Yorkshire' it looks in contrast with such as Bramham Park and Harewood, though now, sadly perhaps, its windows, like theirs, are – just windows.

There is a fine view of Otley from the Chevin which rises nearly 900 feet south of the town: the 'Surprise View', they call it, though to me the surprise is that the rusty gasometer at the heart of the little town, spread out far below, has been allowed to survive to disfigure it. Having had my grumble, let me add with all speed that I like Otley – a necessary bit of diplomacy since I spend a great deal of my time there.

I like the narrow, cobbled streets and the market (probably older than its charter of 1222, granted by Henry II) which packs quite a few of those streets every Friday; I like the country town atmosphere created by the melancholy voices of cattle as they are taken to and from the cattle market; I like the sturdy church with its Norman chancel, and the presence of the Wharfe, which raised municipal tennis courts and putting greens to almost Elysian charm simply by running beside them. This is the river into which boys of Prince Henry's Grammar School, named by James I, are supposed to throw their caps on their last day at school. And, like thousands more, I regard Otley Show, held every year in May, with the sort of veneration due to the oldest agricultural show of its kind in England.

Otley, to my mind at least, has the feel of the Dales about it; yet it is very much a West Riding town in its combination of agriculture and industry – famous for the printing machinery made here, notably the aptly named 'Wharfedale' press.

Otley can be a busy and noisy place, whose older residents regret the passing of the quiet town, while rejoicing that you can still find 'little surprises round every corner' – such as the tiny museum, repository for relics prized by Otley families for generations – like a nineteenth-

century magistrate's staff or a bar counter fly trap. There is a road called
Birdcage Walk and the Jubilee clock, which commemorates Victoria's
reign. Did Otley, I wonder, celebrate *her* Jubilee with a beacon on top of
the Chevin, as they did the Jubilee of 1977? In the market place there
stands the Buttercross – though it is more of a shelter with seats than a
cross – where farmers long enjoyed their medieval right to display their
produce, and exercised it until 1939.

But if Otley had none of the delights I here extol, it would still have a
unique fame as the birthplace of the 'Shakespeare of cabinet-makers' –
Thomas Chippendale. How proper that Otley's famous man is
remembered for what he *made* and that hardly anything else is known
about him – except that he was certainly baptised at Otley Parish
Church on 5 June 1718. The son of a carpenter, he had the good fortune
to be nephew to a schoolmaster and it was from him that Thomas had his
earliest lessons before he became a grammar school boy at Prince
Henry's.

He is said to have learned the rudiments of his trade while assisting his
father, whose services were frequently required by the owners of the
great houses in the area. At Nostell Priory, near Wakefield, there is a
large doll's house filled with miniature eighteenth-century furniture of
surpassing beauty, which is traditionally attributed to the young
Chippendale. Some say that Edwin Lascelles, the future builder of
Harewood House, encouraged Thomas to develop his skill in London.
(Or could it be true that he ventured south because he could not hit it off
with his father's second wife?) Anyway, for whatever reason, London got
him, and, like so many Yorkshiremen before and since, he soon made his
mark in the capital – at least where fashionable furniture-making was
concerned. He reigned for many a year at the sign of The Chair in St
Martin's Lane. The boy from Otley who is remembered as one of the
greatest of English furniture-makers has left abundant memorials in his
native county and particularly at Harewood House and Nostell Priory,
where he worked to themes originated by Robert Adam.

What do the 'ordinary' folk of Otley think of this illustrious son of
their town? There was a time when two plaques, one bearing a
representation of a Chippendale chair, on the site of his supposed
birthplace, and one on the Old Grammar School in Manor Square,
were perhaps the only signs of his connection with the little town beside
the Wharfe. Otley has been taken to task more than once for its presumed neglect – though the charge could well have proved unfair if put
to the test; Otley folk are no more given to fussing than anyone else in
Yorkshire.

However, any hurt feelings on the part of Thomas's shade were surely
salved 250 years after his birth, for that was when a ride of trees was
planted in memory of him on the Chevin. I hope he approves of this

delightful memorial: he should, for after all his life was lived in the closest company with wood. Or does the spirit of this man who resigned from the Royal Society of Arts because he found himself listed as a plain mister (everyone else seemed to be an 'esquire') take greater pleasure in the existence of an international society, formed in 1963 and dedicated to his remembrance?

North of Otley lies the Washburn Valley, through which the River Washburn creates a miniature lake district of reservoirs as it runs its 15-mile course from the boggy wastes of Pockstones Moor.

Dinghy sails now add colour to the Thruscross Reservoir, where flax mills and a corn mill once provided jobs for the 'rude people' who had to win their bread in humbler ways than the yeoman families of this little dale – the Parkinsons, Thackerays and Fairfaxes. Beneath that reservoir lies West End Church, drowned in the cause of reservoir-making: another church now stands above the waterline.

The other reservoirs of Fewston, Swinsty and Lindley Wood mark the course of the river flowing towards Farnley, with its hall and its memories of Turner, who often stayed there as the guest of Squire Fawkes. Turner paintings are still housed at Farnley, to which the young artist came to make drawings for Dr Whitaker's detailed *History of Craven* (and according to one story, to use Otley Chevin as 'the Alps' in a painting of Hannibal's feat of military mountaineering).

The Fawkes family are as much a part of Wharfedale as were the Cromwellian Fairfaxes. At Farnley Hall there is a little stone garden table at which Cromwell is said to have planned the Battle of Marston Moor with Thomas Fairfax and his uncle Charles.

Thomas (Black Tom) Fairfax, who became Third Baron Fairfax of Cameron and Commander-in-Chief of Cromwell's New Model Army, was born at Denton Hall between Otley and Ilkley. His nickname has no sinister connotation. It refers simply to his swarthy complexion, for Tom's character was as noble as his appearance was comely. He was loved by women as well as the men who fought with him in the cause he firmly believed was as much God's as his own.

Denton Hall (rebuilt in the eighteenth century) is happily placed. From Otley a quiet narrow road runs to Ilkley and Bolton Bridge, parallel with the busy main road, but separated from it by the Wharfe. Little more than a gentle country lane, it passes through Weston and Askwith until, after two miles, it reaches Black Tom's birthplace, on the right.

He was the son of Ferdinando and Lady Mary Fairfax and his mother died in childbirth when he was seven, leaving him the eldest of nine children. Tom was cherished by his grandfather. 'Tom, Tom, mind thou the battles', the old man is reported to have said. The formidable old Puritan had already lost three of his sons in continental wars and he naturally feared to lose his grandson – as well he might, for 'Fiery Tom' (another of his nicknames) gave early indication of his dashing nature.

But brave though he proved to be in action during the Thirty Years War, he was a gentle character, tall and slender and afflicted with a rather pathetic stammer. Nor was he robust: he had contracted fever in the Netherlands and as if that were not enough, suffered also from the stone and gout.

He fought in Scotland, too, though characteristically he added his voice to an appeal against taking trained bands out of England. In 1639 the heart of his grandfather must have rejoiced when Tom was knighted. When, in the following year, the old man died, he left his title to his son, but his best horse and best arms to his grandson Tom.

Had the old man lived longer he would have known still greater pride in seeing his beloved Tom rise brilliantly during the Civil War, from which he emerged with a reputation enhanced by his consistent gallantry. It was Tom who saved York Minster's priceless stained glass during the siege of York, and offered rewards for the recovery of monastic manuscripts salvaged from the rubble of St Mary's Tower.

He would have nothing to do with trying the King after the war. Indeed, at the trial, Thomas's wife, who had shared so many of her husband's perils in the field, raised her voice in protest. But to no avail; so Tom and his wife retired to his newly built house at Nun Appleton, near Tadcaster, to live peacefully among his books, coins and medals, emerging after the collapse of the Commonwealth to secure the restoration of Charles II.

On the way from Otley to Ilkley you pass Burley-in-Wharfedale, and the Malt Shovel Inn, where, beneath the Pudding Tree, a huge pudding of pastry and fruit used to be served on the annual feast day to all who cared to share it.

Perhaps Job Senior was one who did, though Job lived not at Burley, but at the breezy hamlet of Burley Woodhead on the edge of Ilkley Moor – a place so small you might easily miss it if you did not look out for the Hermit Inn with its vivid sign depicting the hermit himself, a ragged figure whose story is as strange and pathetic as his picture.

Born in 1780, Job had the gift of being able to sing treble, alto, tenor and bass. He acquired considerable local fame, but when the girl of his choice rejected him, turned to drink. And the more he drank, the stranger became his appearance. He wore a ragged coat patched in a wonderful variety of colours, a brimless hat from which dangled his pipe on a string. He stuffed his clogs with straw for he had no socks, though his rheumatism was so acute that he needed sticks to enable him to walk.

Job's second attempt at matrimony was even more disastrous than the first. He was 60 when he proposed to Judy Barrett and she was 80 (with a nice cottage on the edge of the moor). He told her she was a bonny lass and she succumbed to his flattery. Sadly their marriage was short-lived, for Judy fell ill and, according to one story, told Job she could fancy a nice bit o' roast bacon, whereupon he gave her hot bacon fat instead, with the result that she died of a burnt stomach. The hapless Job blamed himself, especially since Judy had left all her possessions to him. When her infuriated relatives tore down the cottage and stole Job's savings, he built from the remains a tiny shelter which he had to enter on hands and knees. And there he stayed, acquiring a widespread reputation as a weather prophet and an expert on love and marriage, consulted by the lovelorn young men of the district, to whom his advice was apparently always the same: 'Don't do it – a wife an' bairns eat brass like maggots eat cheese.' He died of cholera at 77.

Ilkley Moor, upon which Job must have looked many times, is almost as much a mixture, in its way, of the comic and strange as Job himself! To start with the comic, it is the subject of Yorkshire's so-called 'anthem'.

This rousing ditty, sung to the hymn tune *Cranbrook*, unites Yorkshiremen the world over at least as effectively as the Red Flag unites Socialists. And despite the somewhat primitive humour which permeates it and which gave it birth, it is sung with the greatest ceremony at such august gatherings as the annual dinners of the Society of Yorkshiremen in London – no matter how distinguished the guests. Be they archbishops or prime ministers, if Yorkshiremen, they are expected to join in, and join in they do – with enthusiasm or embarrassment according to their natures.

Such solemnity would surely convulse the creators of the anthem, traditionally a West Riding choir visiting Ilkley and its Moor sometime in the nineteenth century, who flung decorum to the winds as they added stanza to stanza while riding, perhaps, in an open charabanc on their annual outing.

Wheer 'as tha been sin' Ah saw thee?

it begins, or as our more polite southern friends might put it, 'Where have you been since I saw you last?' I will spare you the full version. Summarised, it tells the story of a reckless youth who, having been so ill-advised as to go courting baht 'at (hatless) on Ilkley Moor is in danger of catching a fatal chill and thereafter being eaten by the worms, which will be devoured in turn by the ducks, those same ducks being consumed in due course by his fellow choir-members.

.   *Then we shall all have etten thee*

declares the final chorus with zestful gloom.

Could there be an element of historicity here, or is it merely fanciful to speculate about the true story behind the existence of Cowper's Cross, which stands near the track leading over the moor to Keighley? Cowper, or cooper, was an old name for a pedlar and the one whose grave the cross may mark is supposed to have perished here in a blizzard. The mere thought strikes enough of a chill to make me resolve to buy a hat.

But enough of such levity! Ilkley Moor deserves serious treatment. Its 'proper' name, by the way of Rombald's Moor, Rombald having been one of those giants much given, in times past, to hurling mountains about.

More probable, if hardly less mysterious beings left their mark on the moor – men of the Bronze and Iron Ages whose stone markings include a swastika which owes nothing to Hitler or the Nazis – it tell us that when these early Yorkshiremen watched the sun rise on Ilkley Moor, they were witnessing the ascension of their deity, for they were fire-worshippers, and they trod the Ilkley ground 800 years before Christ walked in the Holy Land.

But the best known rocks on Ilkley Moor are undoubtedly the Cow and Calf, the 'cow' being worth climbing for the view you get from the top. A stony place this moor, with its Rocky Valley, its Panorama Rocks, the Pancake Rock and Doubler Stones on Addingham Moorside. . . . And not at all the featureless place it may sound, fit only to be wandered upon, hatless, by those with nothing better to do.

Another relic of those Bronze- and Iron-Age men is the great Greenbank Earthwork half a mile in length and 50 feet wide. The moor has a tarn, too, which is home to water fowl, and at White Wells there are baths which reputedly date back to Roman times and which in the eighteenth century enjoyed a reputation for very remarkable cures for a variety of ailments including 'the abuse of liquors and effects arising from late hours'.

The Romans, whether or not they knew White Wells, certainly knew Ilkley, though they called it Olicana. At the rear of All Saints Church is a fragment of the station the legions established here, while two of their altars were doubtless surprised to find themselves built into the old church's unquestionably orthodox church tower. As surprised as Hercules, possibly, whose temple may once have occupied this site. Perhaps an even stranger juxtaposition is that of Ilkley's other Anglican church, the splendid St Margaret's, with three 'cup and ring' stones in a public garden opposite, which were found about a mile away on the moor and brought to this spot. One of them measures 15 feet by 12 feet.

Just what do they mean, the markings on these stones in homely Ilkley, which, so the guide books tell us occur on stones as far away from Wharfedale as the Fiji Islands, Palestine or the U.S.A.? Whether they indicate a sepulchre or are an early almanac of astronomical activity, there seems little doubt that whoever inscribed these markings saw the sun as his divinity.

Despite such attractions, early visitors to Ilkley were hardly impressed. The town which was described by a Dr Richardson in 1709 as dirty and insignificant had apparently changed little by the late 1830s, when a Dr Granville found it 'a primitive and simple village' – though by this time it contained some lodging houses and had apparently become a holiday place of sorts.

Then came the Age of the Hydros, when wealthy seekers after health arrived in Ilkley in such numbers that those lodging houses proved inadequate. In 1840 a former mayor of Leeds opened his own 'hydropathic establishment' and called it Ben Rhydding, presumably because he had found on an old map a field named *Beau* Ridding. Another of the hydros, Wells House, was designed by Cuthbert Brodrick, the architect of Leeds Town Hall. Wells House is now a college for housecraft teachers and Ben Rhydding, after a varied career, has been demolished; its name surviving as that of the community which developed around it.

But the Hydro Age and the coming of the railway in 1865 did their work for Ilkley. Without the little mid-Wharfedale town's Victorian fame those nineteenth-century choristers might have chosen a different destination for their outing and Yorkshire's anthem might celebrate, say, Penyghent or Flamborough Head. And yet it could be argued that Ilkley, by reason of its situation in idyllic Wharfedale, would have achieved fame with or without hydros: there would still have been the Elizabethan manor house behind the church, though whether it would have been restored in 1961 and would now house a museum of Roman and other relics from Olicana's past, as well as an art gallery, who can say? Certainly the Manor House was here long before the hydros and will no doubt continue to survive them with no discernible effort, even if its most important days are long past. For Ilkley is now – sadly, to some of us – part of the Bradford Metropolitan District and its affairs are no longer administered here, where the Lord of the Manor used to hold his Court Baron and Court Leet; and where the old house remained the seat of administrative authority until the Local Board bought the manorial rights in 1893.

Bolton Abbey is one of the best-loved names in Yorkshire, though apart from the village which bears that name there is strictly no such thing. For the 'Abbey' is actually a priory – or was, until the Dissolution. The surrender took place on 29 January 1538, and the doubtless heavy-hearted Prior Moone who gave up the keys to King Hal's officers, and who had presumably supervised the building of its western tower, may well have wondered if at some future time that half-finished tower might yet reach completion. But of course it never did. Instead, stone from the dismantled buildings became materials for Bolton Hall, the Yorkshire home of the Duke of Devonshire.

It was the custom of an earlier Duke, by the way, to entertain his tenants once a year at the hall – an event which may well have proved a mixed pleasure to some of them. One such was the widow, unaccustomed to the finer points of etiquette, who drank the contents of her finger bowl. The footman, hiding his grins, refilled it. Again she emptied it; again a servant filled it. And though she protested, 'Tha'll bust me!' she emptied it yet once more. Asked later how she had enjoyed the event, she replied: 'All reight – till it came t' watter course.'

Dalesfolk are not easily overawed, but the hall, which incorporates the three-storeyed priory gatehouse with its four towers, must have seemed an imposing structure to those who visited it once a year. Today, I suppose, guests rarely drink from their finger bowls when the present Duke entertains guests who come up for the shooting in August. . . . A pity, perhaps.

Built, like Bolton Hall, from the stone bones of the Priory is the rectory (once a grammar school) which incorporates the infirmary's original six-light window.

Was it chance, circumstance or someone's superb taste in scenery that made the Augustinian canons first choose their perfect site, with its blend of river, moorland and woodland, after their secession from the Cistercian Order?

William de Meschines and his wife Cecily de Romilly had first endowed the priory, at Embsay, in 1120. So perhaps it was their daughter Alice who, 30 years later, not only granted but herself chose the site to which the Priory was now transferred. It was finished in about 1220. Today, only the nave and the aisle of the Priory church, dedicated to the Blessed Virgin and the North Country's own St Cuthbert, remain intact to serve as the local parish church.

George Edmund Street restored this Early English Church, with its splendid west front, in 1880. The rest of the priory is a mixed museum of architectural styles representing the four centuries of the Priory's life, centuries during which Thomas à Becket died at the mistaken behest of an earlier King Henry; the Black Death scourged England; the Wars of the Roses brought the first Tudor king to the English throne, and the lords of nearby Beamsley were brought here when they died and buried upright beneath its stones.

Watch for spectres when you visit Bolton Abbey (and nothing so commonplace, either, as the phantom monks you might expect – though these, too, of course, have often enough been seen). I refer now to ghosts on four legs, the white spectral animals of Bolton – the doe of Rylstone, which still haunts the ruins and the White Horse of Wharfedale which rises from the surging waters a mile or two up-stream, whenever the Strid claims a victim.

Both are associated with legends of death and disaster. 'The White Doe of Rylstone', which inspired Wordsworth's poem of that name, was the beloved companion of Emily Norton, the gift of her brother Francis, who, along with others of his family, died for his Catholic faith in the Rising of the North in 1569. The Protestant Emily alone is said to have survived, and when she journeyed from the family home at Rylstone to pray at her brother's tomb at the priory, the gentle animal walked by her side. She died, it is said, of sorrow and the doe is still seen from time to time, searching for her tragic mistress.

Made of much sterner stuff is the White Horse of the Strid, first conjured maybe, by an imagination whisked into fantasy by the foaming waters which threaten all but the most wary.

The Strid . . . a notorious name with a sombre reputation which ill accords with the peaceful beauty of its surroundings. It means a stride and it describes the gorge barely more than a yard in width through which the Wharfe pours between smooth and slippery rocks. Narrow it may be, but it is also deep, probably all of 30 feet, and the currents have been deadly to many who have tried to jump across – it looks so easy – and slipped back on reaching the other side to be sucked beneath the swirling stream.

Few indeed have escaped after falling into the Strid and one of those, ironically, was a would-be suicide!

According to legend, it was an early Strid fatality which brought about the very existence of the Priory. The 'Boy of Egremond', of Wordsworth's poem 'The Force of Prayer', was the son of Alice de Romilly, whose parents, you recall, endowed the first priory at Embsay. Returning home from hunting, full of youthful high spirits, with his hound on a lead, he would have gaily leapt the Strid, but the hound hung back and so the boy's leap fell short and he was drowned.

Legend said that in her sorrow his mother founded the Bolton community, but since the boy's name appears on the Priory's foundation deeds that can hardly be true.

Neither the 'Boy' nor his parents could have dreamed that their pious benefactions would be appreciated by countless walkers long after the last of the priory's canons had gone to his reward. There are splendid walks through the woods to the Valley of Desolation, once the scene of a spectacular storm; to Park Waterfall, 50 feet high, and a smaller fall further up the valley. Simon's Seat, rears its craggy head almost 1,600 feet.

You may walk, too, to Barden Tower with its memories of Henry

Clifford, the 'Shepherd Lord', who converted it from a keeper's lodge in 1485. (It was Lady Anne Clifford who restored the building in the seventeenth century, just as she restored Skipton Castle, where Henry was born.)

In 1461, after the Battle of Towton in which the Cliffords supported the House of Lancaster, news came to Skipton that the Yorkists were victorious and that Lord Clifford was dead from an arrow in his throat.

Fearing the Yorkists' vengeance, Lady Clifford and her children left the castle, then separated and went into hiding. Henry went to live among shepherds in a lonely part of Cumberland, returning after many years when it was safe for the Cliffords to reign again from Skipton Castle in all their old pomp. But after his years of humble life, such splendour had no appeal for Henry, which is why he made himself a simpler house in the forest of Barden. He fought with distinction at Flodden Field when he was 60, and ten years later joined his ancestors in Bolton Church.

Near Barden Tower a road leads off to Appletreewick and Trollers Ghyll, a limestone valley shaped like a twisted, elongated basin with outcropping limestone on its sides and a stream running through. There is a sense of quiet and remoteness here, but the ghyll clearly holds no terrors for the picnickers who relax in its peace. All of which goes to show how differently we react from our forebears. For them, the enclosing hillsides were threatening; imprisoning, rather than protecting, as we probably find them, from the clamorous world of today. But we, too, might feel less secure if, denied an easy escape route by comfortable car, we found ourselves benighted in the ghyll with only the creatures of our imagination for company . . . such as, for instance, a giant hound named the Barguest.

Legends of spectral hounds are to be found everywhere – in Wales, Norfolk, Derbyshire, Devonshire. . . . They have different names, of course – Sky Dog, Gabriel Hound, Hell Dog. But you laugh at them at your peril! John Lambert did. He laughed loud and long with his bar-room cronies then went to the ghyll to 'tak' on t' barguest'. Evidence of the encounter was found next morning in the great wounds across John's chest – but there was no point in asking his corpse how they came there. . . .

Billy Blakey was luckier. 'Git up an' stir thysel', he told the saucer-eyed beast when he arrived home at Linton to find it staring up at him from the doorstep. It remained where it was until it heard the firm footsteps of Billy's wife as she came to open the door to her boozy husband. Wise dog? Even a barguest must know when it has met its match. . . .

Near the entrance to the ghyll is Parcevall Hall, whose present use as a church conference centre must make one of its ghosts distinctly uneasy – that of John ('Swift Nick') Nevison, the roving highwayman who hid there and whose fame in Yorkshire may well have outshone Dick Turpin's.

The view of Burnsall from the road up Wharfedale must be one of the most photographed in all Yorkshire. There is the graceful five-arched bridge, the river winding through lush pastures and, behind the bridge, clustered cottages and church rising against a backcloth of woodland and then the bare fells. All this tells me that now at last I am in Wharfedale. Otley and Ilkley may be only a round dozen miles or so behind, but already there is a different taste in the air. Ahead lies delight in the increasing wildness of the dale as the road climbs towards the Wharfe's birthplace.

That church, so perfectly sited, links Burnsall with its ancient past: even the font bears pagan Norse symbols to match the carved Viking tombstones. They may have resembled a 'hog's back' to our more recent ancestors, but were meant to represent a Danish house, carved with tiles or slates and with dragon-like heads at their ends. They take us back to the Burnsall of a thousand years ago and even then are not as old as the memories enshrined in the church's dedication; for St Wilfrid, whose name it bears, was Abbot at Ripon in 671. A wild place Burnsall must have been when, as history records, he visited it. Certainly the church he may have seen here bore little resemblance to the present one (first rebuilt by the Normans). But William Craven knew this church a millenium later and 'butified' it, as he did Burnsall itself.

In 1602 he built the lovely Tudor-style grammar school, now the village school, next to the church, and Burnsall has him to thank, too, for rebuilding the bridge which forms so large a part of its charm.

Wharfedale's own Dick Whittington, Sir William was 'Lord Mayre' of London in 1598 but he never forgot either his beloved Burnsall or Appletreewick, where he was born in 1548 in a cottage, now part of St John's Church. William was 13 when he was sent to London by carrier's cart to be bound apprentice to a tailor. By the time he was 21 he had become a member of the Merchant Taylors' Guild and at 50 was chief citizen of the capital, having already served it as alderman and sheriff. At High Hall, where he lived on his return to 'Aptrick', a fine carved oak minstrel gallery looks down on the banqueting hall. For company there is ancient Monks Hall, on whose site lived monks in charge of Bolton Priory's property hereabouts.

Sir William is not the only Wharfedale worthy commemorated by a panel in Burnsall Church. There is Robert Heye, one-time school-master, who died in 1694 in his thirty-sixth year and whose memorial was placed here by his dutiful young son (though I suspect – indeed hope – someone lent a hand with its composition):

'Beneath your feet lies all that came from the ground of Robert Heye, M.A. (if thou coolest not his warm ashes with thy tear, yet mayest thou tread lightly upon his tomb) who, born in the neighbouring parts, ruled for 12 years the school hard by the church's graveyard in a way which was worthy equally of Sparta, while he cultivated the minds and morals of his pupils by expending in care and teaching not only the agreed hours of the same school but his leisure moments in other hours . . . to his memory, his sorrowful surviving son John Heye of Skierhome commands and vows this memorial of his father's love'. . . . I wonder how his pupils saw him.

Halliwell Sutcliffe, the Dales novelist who lived a little way updale at Linton, tells a lovely story in *The Striding Dales* of the theft of the Burnsall maypole. One spring morning the villagers awoke to find a staggering situation. The maypole which last night had reared proudly above the village green was there no more.

Who could have taken it? Only the devil, some opined, would have the necessary blend of power and wickedness. Others nodded sagely and suggested that more than one devil was responsible and they all came from Aptrick, where such antics were thought amusing – especially if the victim was Burnsall.

A search party went to Appletreewick, but found no maypole. Nor was it at Barden or Hebden or Linton. 'Let's try Cracoe', said someone, but on the way they saw from the hilltop the golden tip of their maypole glinting from the secluded village of Thorpe-in-the-Hollow.

With the fury, if not the numbers, of Sennacherib's horde, the Burnsall men descended on Thorpe – to find the people equally indignant at the mysterious presence on *their* green of a maypole they had apparently neither stolen nor wanted. But the Burnsall men were hard to convince. There was only one way to settle it, and after the long, hard battle, with honour satisfied, the contestants shared a picnic, before Burnsall and Thorpe men together, carried off the maypole to replant it in its rightful home.

In Linton churchyard the sound of sheep dutifully cropping the grass is sometimes all there is to hear – apart from the wind in the trees or the stony music of the Wharfe on whose west bank rests the long, low church.

An unassuming church this, and without a tower. You would hardly think it served perhaps the biggest parish in the Dales, comprising Grassington, Linton, Threshfield and Hebden – but with its lowly beauty it need not be assertive.

It stands a mile away from Linton at the end of the Low Mill road; and nearby you may cross the river by stepping-stones and walk across the fields to Hebden, though I for one prefer to linger, as the church itself – or most of it – has done for six centuries. Now it blends Early English with Early Norman styles and links the lovely area it serves with its long history. In relation to that history, the churchyard seat in memory of Halliwell Sutcliffe might have been presented a mere half hour ago by the admiring Association of Yorkshire Bookmen.

Sutcliffe lived in Linton itself, at White Abbey, a house around which his novelist's fancy loved to weave. He died in 1933, but perhaps the *Somebody*, whose influence he claimed to feel in the house remains there still. *Somebody* - at least for Sutcliffe - was associated with White Abbey's past, which reaches back as far as the days when monks of Fountains Abbey rested there while journeying on the Abbey's business. But over the centuries, Cistercian simplicity gave way to the comparative comfort of what is basically a seventeenth-century yeoman's house, despite the nineteenth-century additions at the back.

Sutcliffe it was who restored the old name White Abbey, which had been changed to Troutbeck. He believed there was a priest hole here, because a corner of his study was of greater width than the room below and the difference hard to account for. There must be a hidden room there, eight feet high and six feet square, he concluded, but he never tried to find it - for fear, maybe, of offending *Somebody?*

White Abbey has a shy look behind its beeches and sycamores - they say a former parson owner laid stepping stones to its garden gate so that he might come and go without traversing the village. Across that stream, the fine Georgian-fronted Linton House is similarly retiring among the trees.

Perhaps they feel overawed by the most impressive building in Linton, a memorial of Richard Fountaine, who built it. He was yet another who somehow made the then almost astronomical journey from the Dales to London in the seventeenth century and returned a rich man to endow this, the Fountaine Hospital, in 1721. It was the time of the Great Plague - but a Yorkshireman can turn anything to good account. He caught the plague himself, but recovered and made a fortune by disposing of the victims for the government, who were understandably grateful for help with the melancholy problem. His hospital was to house six poor men or women, and some say Sir John Vanbrugh, the architect of Castle Howard, drew its miniature lines. The central block, surmounted by a square tower and a cupola contains a chapel, tiny and beautiful, whose Venetian east window frames a view of the fells.

Fountaine is remembered, too, in the name of the inn. His Georgian hospital blends happily with this and Linton's other buildings - White Abbey, Linton House, the Old Hall, the former rectory, now a youth hostel, and the old post office dating back to 1679.

The one discordant note - in my view at least - is the prize won by Linton in 1949 in a competition organised by the old *News Chronicle* for the 'Loveliest Village in the North' - an astrolabe mounted, somewhat incongruously, I felt, on a section of fluted column from London's Northumberland House, damaged by German bombs during the war.

The pillar stands on the village green, which is divided by the Linton Beck, spanned by three bridges - a modern road bridge, a fourteenth-century packhorse bridge and an ancient clapper bridge with added railings; there is also a ford and the stepping stones. No difficulty, as you can see, in getting across.

In its formation typical enough, with buildings set around a central green, Linton was once, less typically, a textile village. On your way to Linton church you pass a line or two of cottages called Botany, from Botany wool. They were built in the mid-nineteenth century as homes for workers at Linton Mill, a rebuilt corn mill, where cotton was woven. After a spell as a creamery, followed by a fire, it reverted to textiles until it was closed in 1959.

Strange to think that the glacial action which moulded the features of the Dales also set Linton on the textile track. As the Ice Age ended, glacial debris dammed Linton Beck, forming a lake (long since drained) and eventually this became a marsh, which was perfect for flax growing. A musical name, Linton - well suited to 'the North's prettiest village' - but it simply means a place where flax is grown.

Not quite so mellifluous, the name Threshfield means - as you might well guess - 'the place where threshing takes place'! Linton's travelling companion up Wharfedale, Threshfield, too, recalls Anglian times, though my favourite Threshfield building - the Free Grammar School (some distance from the actual village and now a primary school) dates only from 1674, when it was founded and endowed by a Rector of Linton, Matthew Hewitt, who also in his will left £12 10s. a year to educate four scholars of St John's College, Cambridge.

Halliwell Sutcliffe, who could walk from his garden gate and cross the beck by stepping stones to the holly-bordered path which leads across the old railway to Threshfield, wrote about that village's ghost. Old Pam, it would seem, was Threshfield's schoolmaster - and an obsessive fiddler. Stranger still, he met his death at the surprisingly murderous hands of a rector of Linton, a predecessor, perhaps, of the bashful cleric who laid those stepping stones, and who was himself addicted to dancing jigs as his butler fiddled - with his back respectfully turned. A captivating player he must have been, to have persuaded his solemn master to indulge in such unseemly antics! But compared with the fiddling of Old Pam's ghost, his music was tameness itself.

Not all Linton rectors were fond of the fiddle. Indeed, it was because Pam played too often for one rector's liking, at fairs and inns and weddings, that they came to blows and in his self-righteous fury the cleric fought too fiercely and poor Pam fell dead beneath his blows – to be buried by that same grief-stricken rector. Or so it has been recorded.

But even death could not silence Pam's fiddle. Villagers passing the school at midnight saw candles burning and peered up through the windows of the room above the porch to see his ghost fiddling for an audience of imps, and dancing, like them, to his own music.

One nocturnal observer was misguided enough to sneeze, whereupon Old Pam and his goblin friends gave chase and only let him be when he found safety by jumping into the Lady Well. That well still runs today, though it no longer provides water for the cottages hereabouts. One of the oldest of the dwellings here takes its name from that stream – Lady Well Cottage, built in 1603.

A pity that not all Threshfield's historic dwellings have survived. . . . In the time of James I a moss-trooper and border cattle-rustler named Ibbotson swaggered or slunk into the village, having had his fill of fighting, and set up as a besom-maker, turning out good brooms in such abundance that he soon made a name for himself and for Threshfield. His descendants continued in the craft until the last of them died in 1926. Their home was Ling House near the bridge. Fire destroyed it and a modern house now occupies the site. It, too, is called Ling House.

A shy place, Threshfield, all too easily overlooked by travellers to and from Skipton. The stocks on the tiny triangular village green, called The Park (what remains of it) are hardly noticeable among the surrounding trees. Across the road is the Old Hall Inn, a·comparative youngster despite its name, for it is largely eighteenth century, though its outbuildings include part of Threshfield's original Old Hall, dating possibly to the fourteenth century.

But for the tarmac road with its phone box, quarry lorries and visitors' cars, the heart of old Threshfield might still belong to an earlier century. Of its handful of houses a surprising number proudly announce their antiquity, like Park Grange, whose datestone reads 1640, between the initials F and H.

'*Ja, Emmerdale Farm!*' said the *Hausfrau* on holiday as a familiar image caught her eye in a Grassington bookshop. It demonstrated the sort of interchange which now takes place between the once-remote and hidden Dales and the world beyond. Some critics may sneer at Yorkshire Television's Dales serial, calling it 'Coronation Street with grass', but this saga of the Sugden family and their fellow Dales-folk proves by its hold on 'the viewing public' that most of us remain countrymen at heart. And no-one, surely, could honestly quarrel with that (unless he were trying to park his car in Grassington's square on a fine Saturday afternoon).

Nor do all Grassington visitors come, like the *Hausfrau*, from Europe, you are quite as likely to bump into a solemn procession of dark-skinned dignitaries being introduced to Grassington as a classic among Yorkshire villages; or Scandinavians seeking lager in the Devonshire Hotel.

On one of my recent visits the Devonshire was staging an exhibition of paintings by Neil Wingate, one of the élite body of artists dedicated, in the tradition of Fred Lawson and Angus Rands to reproducing with paint and canvas that endless variety of sky and weather which might be said to be the only constant factor of the Dales.

It was a typically busy Grassington day, but you had only to leave the main street (climbing steeply until suddenly it runs out of cafés and shops and loses itself on Hebden Moor) to find the old, little-changing Grassington – all 'folds' of stone cottages with paradisal gardens. You feel a certain sympathy for the inhabitants of such cottages and the tenders of such gardens when you read notices such as this one near the approach to the village:

This is not the Rectory.
We do not keep the keys of the church.
We do not make teas.
The way to Grassington is past the mill and over the bridge.
The way to Burnsall is over the stepping stones.

It could be said to combine courtesy, firmness and helpfulness with a sort of restrained desperation!

Grassington's little folk museum gives tangible expression to the love with which the past of the town, and indeed of Wharfedale itself, has been preserved in defiance of transistor radios outside and the motor coaches straining up the sloping main street. Here, an old-fashioned gramophone squeaks out bygone hits as an accompaniment to your reading of *An Appreciation of Halliwell Sutcliffe* from *Great Thoughts*, whose faded pages help to paper the wall. Sutcliffe would surely rejoice in this fond conglomeration of bygones; but which, I wonder among the exhibits would stimulate his novelist's imagination the most?

Sutcliffe found his own sort of 'gold' here, a rich seam of life and character which gave him raw material for his books; but the Dales have produced another kind of gold, like that contained in a phial in the Grassington museum, a whole ounce of it, in grains panned from streams further up-dale around Kettlewell in about 1930 and valued in those days at around £4. But writers are generally more interested in people than even the concept of a Kettlewell Klondike! And Sutcliffe's fancy may well have proved more responsive to the drenching horns and knife found in 1936 in the smithy of the man whose name used to send shivers down the spines of honest Grassington folk.

Lee's Smithy (or smiddy) is still in Grassington: the metal plate on the wall of a fruit shop in the main street informs you of its bygone function. Lee, the violent and hot-tempered blacksmith, had no doubt drunk more than was good for him on the night he met Dr Petty at a Kilnsey inn, and the well-loved doctor warned him to mend his ways. Nursing his hatred, Lee lay in wait for the doctor at the north end of Grass Woods, and when the physician passed by on his homeward way, sprang upon him and beat him to the ground.

'Ah've *done* for 'im!' he may have boasted, when, still not quite sober, he told the story back at the smiddy to his wife and his unfortunate apprentice, Jack Sharp.

'Ho'd yer tongue, Tom', his wife must surely have replied, with a warning glance at the lad.

'What? Oh, I'll see *he* doesn't blab!'

Now three parts sober, Lee is said to have taken his wife and the doubtless reluctant Sharp back to where Petty's body lay. There was still a spark of life there – but not for long. . . .

'Finish 'im . . . Finish 'im,' growled the smith, and poor Jack was too terrified to disobey. He knew that his corpse, too, would lie there if he refused. Now that Sharp's silence was presumably assured, it remained only to dispose of the body. But how? Perhaps fear caused Lee's decision to tremble, for one hiding place after another was tried before he sought one night to consign the body to the Wharfe – above Burnsall – and was espied in the act by two hidden lovers.

Yet although Lee was arrested and tried, he stepped from the dock a free man. Not until years later, after a row at a cockfight at Litton, was the long-suffering Sharp persuaded to tell all he knew to an enemy of Lee who had sworn to see him hanged, as hanged he finally was, at York, though his body was returned to the scene of his crime to hang on a gibbet near Grass Woods as a warning to others.

The Wharfe, you notice, had to get into the tale. It is difficult, in fact, to omit it from any part of Grassington's story. Perhaps the oldest structure in the village, in fact, is the stone river bridge with its mason's marks, which replaced a wooden one in 1603.

There is plenty to notice in Grassington, despite the fact that its population barely tops the thousand: things old as well as new – the rescue post of the Upper Wharfedale Fell Rescue Association, for instance, whose members may be called out at any moment to save some hapless, inexperienced caver or search for a child lost on the moors, where mists fall with terrifying suddenness. There are fine old buildings like the Grassington House Hotel (1760) and the much older Old Hall.

The first settlers in Grassington were Angles who built their huts, perhaps 13 centuries ago, beside the beck which still flows through the village, though now it is covered and unseen. The 'garrs' or enclosures, they made gave the little place its name – Garrston, or Girston, which down the years became 'Grassington'. A reminder of the old name is Garrs Lane in which stands the erstwhile Grassington Theatre, whose boards were trodden by the great Edmund Kean. Today it serves as cottages though it no doubt started life as a barn.

But lead-mining played a bigger part in Grassington life than did any mere 'laikers', as even the most eminent players were probably known. Time was when most of the village men worked in the mines on Grassington high moor. The mining ceased in the early 1880s, but the miners left as a memorial one of the most evocative of place names – Hungry Laugh Hill, for it was from here that their homeward-bound laughter could be heard as they smelt dinner cooking at home.

The prosperity which had vanished from Grassington with the end of lead-mining returned in some measure with the growth of tourism, accelerated by the opening in 1901 of the Yorkshire Dales Railway between Skipton and Grassington. Though the railway has gone, tourism remains a source of work for Grassington folk; whether in hotels, restaurants, or shops, or simply as purveyors of bed and breakfast and sometimes over-whelmingly generous evening meals. It was at Grassington that I was faced at one meal with a joint of beef for two of us that would have fed a family – and with a carving knife and steel to facilitate consumption. After our bravest efforts to 'side' this and the various dishes of trifle and so on, that followed it (to say nothing of cakes and biscuits) we were gently reproved for having 'not eaten much'.

Grassington folk love their village. They were up in arms recently when it was suggested that the old cast-iron parish pump should be re-sited to provide more space for parking in the cobbled square. A local builder said it was too fragile to move and he for one, wouldn't do the job for £1,000! After all, locals recalled, it was another such upheaval that caused injury to poor old Gormless (not, as you might suppose, the village idiot, but a well-loved and ancient lamp).

The easterly road of the two which travel together up this part of Wharfedale leads next to Conistone, where an old bridge links it with the westerly road, with Kilnsey and its crag. One of Wharfedale's unmistakable landmarks, the crag has been likened by the fanciful to a clenched fist and even a monkey's head. Its crown, 165 feet up, overhangs its feet by about 40 feet and affords a fine view for those who climb to the top after following an old road which runs behind the Tennant Arms. This same road crosses to Kilnsey Moor to connect with Mastiles Lane, an old green track, once used by cattle drovers, which leads to Malham with its cove and tarn.

Less than a mile up-dale from Kilnsey Crag the Skirfare joins the Wharfe from Littondale, whose tiny 'capital' is Arncliffe.

Arncliffe is one of those little, hidden places whose charm brings an admiring world to seek out and exhibit them. What could be more retiring, for instance than Littondale itself, the dale of the little River Skirfare, the 'Bright Stream', which runs from Penyghent side south-eastward to join the Wharfe between Kilnsey and Kettlewell. Two thousand feet up on Penyghent flank, the Cosh, Foxup and Crystal Becks are among the many which drain the ghylls and fells and mosses bearing strange and immemorial names – Eller Carr with its Robin Hood's Well, Horse Head Moor, High Bergh, Low Bergh and Far Bergh, not, of course, forgetting Cosh Outside or even Cosh Inside. Few know them, but millions know Arncliffe, if not by that name.

At Foxup, where the Littondale road starts its journey with the Skirfare to the Wharfe, a green road curves west, then south-west round the feet of Penyghent to Horton-in-Ribblesdale. But just now we are concerned with Littondale – or Amerdale as Wordsworth named it, making a choice based on history, unlike Kingsley's – 'The name of the place is Vendale', he wrote in *The Water Babies*, 'and if you want to see it for yourself you must go up into High Craven. . . . A quiet, silent, rich, happy place; a narrow crack cut deep into the earth; so deep and out of the way that the bad bogies can hardly find it out. . . .'

Thus the Victorians. . . . It was inevitable, I suppose, that our own age, too, should discover 'Vendale' – and so Arncliffe was the chosen setting for a television 'wedding of the year' when Joe Sugden, of the bucolic TV series *Emmerdale Farm* was married at St Oswald's.

On that day, extras in country-folk garb thronged the green, a carriage and horses awaited the newly united pair, a mobile canteen stood beside the church and in the village hall, stars, technicians and extras mingled amicably over lunch. And the spirit of the Dales – affronted perhaps, by all this alien activity, protested by allowing the clouds to open as few but Dales clouds can. So it all had to be done again on a more co-operative day.

Two roads take you up the dale, each bordering the Skirfare until they separate at Arncliffe. But the first village you reach after leaving Kilnsey is Hawkswick on the northern side of Littondale's 'bright stream', a neat and tiny hamlet inhabited since Saxon times. Less than two miles north-west of here, Arncliffe rests beside the Skirfare, serenely conscious perhaps that neither Kingsley nor Wordsworth could really improve on its own name, which means 'Eagle Rock'.

It is a village on the ancient pattern – a central green surrounded by stone houses with 'stone slate' roofs. One of those houses at the western end, was a cotton-spinning mill in 1793, with nearly 50 people at work in it. Arncliffe parish extends over 17,000 acres but the village population is about 200. I wonder how many of them are descended from the brave men of the dale who fought at Flodden in 1513 wielding such weapons as the halberd which hangs on the church wall near a list of men and their weapons.

There was John Knolle, 'able horses and harnish'd' (or armoured), Oliver Knolle, his brother, perhaps, who could offer only a 'bowe', while Robert Tylson's weapon was 'a bille'. Altogether, Arncliffe could provide five bowmen and three warriors equipped with 'billes'. The contingent from Hawkswick comprised only two bowmen, William Calvard and Arthur Redyman, but each with 'able horse and harnish'd'. In all, Littondale furnished 22 men with billes and bowes to help 'sort out' the Scots under James IV on that fateful day in 1513. How many returned, I wonder, to worship in the parish church, dedicated to the sainted warrior monarch of whose Northumbrian kingdom Littondale was once a part?

St Oswald's has much to remind itself of its long history – a tuning pipe, for instance, which was used to sound the note for singing before an organ was installed – as late as 1845. In 1619 Margrite Litton (who was doubtless as good as she sounds) presented a chalice inscribed 'A Maiden's Gift'. It was joined in about 1693 by a paten, the gift of Margaret and Agnes Wade. I imagine them as dedicated and elderly maiden sisters. They lived at Kilnsey and were related to that famous General Wade, who 'bid new roads extend' in Scotland, Ireland and elsewhere and may have unknowingly planted ideas in Blind Jack Metcalf's fertile brain, when commanding the army of which the amazing Nidderdale man formed one during the Forty-Five.

Were Arncliffe folk all so estimable? Apparently not! There was the wise woman of Littondale, Bertha, who had something of the reputation of a witch. Rather than meet her face to face, declared G. Bernard Wood in *Yorkshire Villages*, the average villager would take a flying leap over a handy wall. . . .

A mile or two up-dale is Litton, which, since it gives its name to the dale, might be expected to be a good deal more of a place than this collection of farms and cottages, plus the Queen's Arms and a post office which left potential customers in little doubt what they can expect to buy within: 'I do NOT sell bread, butter, tea, ice cream, newspapers, picture postcards. . . .' But another poster redressed the balance by declaring encouragingly: 'I sell sweets, chocolates, cigarettes, tobacco, matches, pop in cans and bottles, crisps. . . .'

The only sound as a young woman led a small child along the snow-muffled village street one day was her impersonations of ducks and dogs and the child's responsive laughter. There was a house bearing on its lintel the initials RA and the date 1734. It is a quiet life in winter in Littondale. A barn door served as a hoarding to advertise a 'film show of local events in Arncliffe Village Hall - silver collection', while someone was holding a coffee evening in aid of Kettlewell Methodist Church.

The next village - 'hamlet' describes it better - as we climb up Littondale, is Halton Gill, over 1,000 feet above sea level; and from here a road south-west affords a grand view of the dale before threading its way between Fountains Fell and Penyghent on its way to Stainforth in Ribblesdale.

After Foxup, too small, almost, to be called a hamlet, the road up Littondale ceases; but a public bridleway leads to Horton-in-Ribblesdale and a track follows the Cosh beck - a parent, like Foxup Beck, of the Skirfare itself - to Cosh, long famous as the loneliest farmhouse in Yorkshire.

Resuming the northward exploration of Wharfedale, you come to Kettlewell, a delightfully jumbled village on the banks of the Cam Beck, which here joins the Wharfe. To the north-east soars Great Whernside's 2,310 feet, as it did when an Irish-Norse chieftain, Ketel, drew water from his well here. Ketel may have bequeathed us only his name - and that a matter not beyond doubt - but the Anglian settlers who lived here left more tangible evidence in the 'lynchets' or ploughing terraces still easily discerned on the lower slopes of the hills.

Kettlewell has long been a busy village, busier indeed than it often is today, when holidaymakers stay at the Bluebell Hotel in which travellers have found rest during three centuries. Or at the Racehorses or the King's Head.

Much of the land hereabouts was once owned by the abbeys of Fountains and Coverham, and moorland roads and tracks - like that into Coverdale, or to Hawkswick or Arncliffe - were often first trodden by monks or miners; for lead was mined here from the mid-1600s until less than a century ago. It seems rather an anti-climax that the present church, in a place with such a history, dates only from 1820.

From Kettlewell, Park Rash, narrow, steep and gated, affords an exhilarating entry to Wensleydale, by way of Coverdale. Near the Rash is Dow Cave, known to present-day troglodytes.

Starbotton lies a mile or two up-dale, and here two artist friends insisted that I stop to allow them to look at the line made by roadside cottage gables - which they did with an excitement rather denied to me. But if I am no artist, at least I knew a little more about the reasons for Starbotton's 'quaintness' than they did. For the village that so enchanted them was laid waste in 1686 by the worst flood ever recorded in the dale. All over England they heard of Starbotton's visitation, and pious folk, who would probably never set foot in Yorkshire, gave their Sunday collection to help the faraway village rebuild as best it could, using whatever came to hand, whether fallen masonry or dislodged river boulders. As might be expected of folk in dire need, they built quickly, their materials fitting at places 'wheer they touched'.

Buckden takes pride in being 'the last village in Wharfedale', for it stands at the point where Langstrothdale soars out over Fleet Moss (1,893 feet) to Hawes in Wensleydale; while Kidstones Pass veers east to Bishopdale (a 'daughter' of Wensleydale) by way of Cray, with its waterfalls. From Kidstones the Stake, a rough fell road, tramps north-west to Semerdale.

Buckden was home to the guardians of Langstrothdale Chase, where Norman lords once hunted the deer which gave Buckden its name. The village sits in the shadow of the 2,302-foot Buckden Pike. Buckden was a bustling place in former times, with three inns. Now there is only one, The Buck, where, long ago, farmers sold their wool to the merchants. Perhaps because the village was once so busy a place, there has always been an audience here for the local musicians and folk dancers who have showed their paces to travellers and fellow dalesfolk.

The first village in Langstrothdale is Hubberholme, whose glory is its Church of St Michael. Here there is one of the only two rood lofts in Yorkshire; this one made by William Jake in 1558 during the reign of the Roman Catholic Mary. Lovingly carved in oak and painted red, black and yellow, it should by all the rules have been destroyed in Protestant Elizabeth's time, yet somehow it survived. A fine craftsman, William would smile today at the tiny mice which show that a more recent Yorkshire wood-carver, Bob Thompson, from Kilburn, was at work here.

Hubberholme's inn, The George, once the vicarage, is the scene of the traditional New Year's Day 'land-letting', or 'Hubberholme Parliament', in which bids are offered for the 'Poor Pasture' left to the village in trust for the benefit of the needy. The Parliament has its 'Lords' (the vicar and churchwardens) and its 'Commons' (the farmers); and their 'proceedings' have been taking place for almost a thousand years. Today the vicar is usually the auctioneer and the benefiting 'poor', old age pensioners.

Hubberholme's strange name is a legacy – or had you guessed? – of yet another Viking, the belligerent Hubba, who found peace here at last, and whose friends settled higher up the valley at Yockenthwaite, Deepdale, Beckermonds.

Bronze Age men left a stone circle at Yockenthwaite; at Beckermonds, as its name implies, the Oughtershaw and Greenfield Becks unite to form the Wharfe. And at Oughtershaw in the last century, the Woodd family built Oughtershaw Hall, which has only the hills and fells for company.

Ahead lies Fleet Moss (1,934 feet), from where a green road that the Romans trod runs below Dodd Fell (2,189 feet) to Cam Houses, one of the loneliest outposts in Yorkshire. Here, in the kingdom of sleeping naked giants, like the Three Peaks and their smaller companions, is the essential glory of the Dales.

FOUR

Haunted Dale of Nidd

T'Owd Man's Kingdom

The Nidd bids us farewell near Nun Monkton, where it joins the Ouse, and no river ever had a sweeter setting for its dying moments. Clearly this is no 'Dales' village in the usual sense. Compared with bleak Middlesmoor, near the start of the river's journey, this gentle place might belong to another country. But for that reason alone it is worth a visit by anyone who seeks to learn the ways of 'Capricious Nidd', as one writer well named the river watering this haunted dale.

Like all the best villages, Nun Monkton encircles a green, and like all good greens, this one contains – besides a maypole – a pond which is home to a multitude of ducks. On the warm summer's day of my last visit, the ducks were keeping well away from two hunters which were being allowed by their riders to cool their fetlocks in the now-muddy water.

But if ducks don't love horses, most Yorkshiremen do. Witness the name of Nun Monkton's village inn, the Alice Hawthorn, which commemorates a much-loved star of the Turf. A faded press cutting on the bar-room wall recalls the numerous victories of the equine lady whose portrait adorns the inn's sign.

Long before Alice made her name, another lady, called Matilda, was here; she was probably the first prioress of the Benedictine house which, if you like, put the 'Nun' in Nun Monkton.

As Domesday Book reveals, this area was first of all called 'Monech-tone', the monech (or monk) being presumably a hermit whose cell stood on the present site of Nun Monkton's beautiful church. After rampaging Vikings had destroyed the cell in the time of Ethelred the Unready, the village was apparently forgotten, to sleep in peace for two centuries. It awoke with an unpleasant start when William the Norman came and gave it to one of his henchmen, Osbern de Arches. He did not take possession without a struggle, for the villagers (domesticated descendants, quite likely, of those marauding Norsemen) rebelled against their new Norman overlord, after which, poor Nun Monkton was almost wiped out in William's reprisals.

It was one of Osbern's descendants, William de Arches, who founded the priory in 1158 to atone, it is said, for his own and his predecessor's sins. Matilda, the first prioress, was his daughter. Nearly four centuries were to pass before the last reverend mother, Joanna Slingsby, and her 15 daughters in God surrendered the priory in 1536 to Henry's agents. Today, the only part of the priory that remains is the nuns' chapel, now the church.

The men who built it in about 1153 were travelling craftsmen who, when they had finished one church or monastery, moved on to the next. And their skill could have no better memorial than this lovely example of Early English church architecture, with its beautiful triforium running along north, south and west walls. In the floor, beneath the large altar table, is the ancient stone altar of pre-Reformation times, one of the best preserved from the period. At each side of the west door there are stone coffin lids, some of which once covered the remains of prioresses.

To reach the church you have to pass along a tree-shaded walk, and even then it seems almost to hide behind a gigantic weeping beech – all of which makes its final discovery the more rewarding.

G. Bernard Wood, in his *Yorkshire Villages*, turns from writing with affection of the beloved village's web-footed inhabitants and the island 'hotel' once provided for them by members of the Women's Institute (tired of finding unsolicited duck eggs in their gardens) to its human residents, past and present. The name of the priory's founder, William de Arches, he finds echoed in the church's architecture. Certainly there is an abundance of arches here, culminating in the three lancets of the nineteenth-century east window by William Morris.

One of the prioresses of Nun Monkton was a daughter of the Slingsbys, who lived across the river at Moor Monkton. Here, at Red House (now a school), the Royalist Sir Henry Slingsby lay in hiding from the Roundheads garrisoned at York until Sir John Bourchier – he lived across the Ouse at Beningborough – shopped him to the Parliamentarians, who executed him on 8 June 1658. A less than neighbourly act, one feels, and ill-befitting such a friendly, smiling landscape.

Charles I slept at Red House in more peaceable days, and the legend survives of a 'secret room' which, so far as I know, keeps its secret still.

Long Marston and Tockwith recall the Battle of Marston Moor on 2 July 1644, when by his victory Cromwell unknowingly won the commemorative obelisk erected in 1938 by his latter-day admirers, the Cromwellian Association. Further west, Cowthorpe was long famed as home to England's 'oldest inhabitant', a gigantic ancient oak, now sadly dead, but splendid still. Described once as the 'largest tree in the kingdom', it has been credited with a life-span of a thousand years, and was even presumed to have been a sapling in Roman times. In 1776, already 'ruinous', it soared 85 feet. Some earlier writers claimed its hollow trunk had contained 70 persons (perhaps – sitting on each other's shoulders, suggested a more cautious reporter).

The old tree was certainly here long before Guy Fawkes came to the village as a boy and became a bell-ringer in the village church. The church at Kirk Hammerton, almost due north of Tockwith, makes a respectable, if less colourful, claim to be Yorkshire's most nearly complete Anglo-Saxon church. It once comprised just chancel, nave and tower, then, in the thirteenth century, acquired a north aisle which in 1891 was absorbed into the new church that Charles Hodgson Fowler built beside the old to provide a most appealing 'church within a church'.

Now the Nidd leaves the oak the Romans may have seen to run beneath the road they undoubtedly made – or rather its successor. I mean, of course, the A1, the Great North Road that used to be. We too must cross that thundering thoroughfare, and be glad, surely, to leave it again to be lost for a time in seeking the unbroken peace of Lower Nidderdale, green and lush, with pan-tiled cottages and rainbow gardens. What a pity it would be to miss all this by seeking only the north-western heights of the Nidd's kingdom!

Driving – not too quickly – along the 6164 you will see to the right the sedate and spacious Ribston Hall, built in 1674. Apple seed brought from Rouen was planted here in 1709 by Sir Henry Goodricke, and the fruit borne in due time was named the Ribston Pippin – progenitor of all the pippins grown in England today. So there are two historic arboreal relics in this leafy neighbourhood – not only the ruined Cowthorpe Oak but the stump of an apple tree lovingly armoured against time with a jacket of lead.

Hardly surprising that men with the means and the money chose to build beautiful, sometimes magnificent, houses here. At Goldsborough is an Elizabethan hall, once the home of the Princess Royal. And in St Mary's Church there, some fine monuments include one of the best effigies in England – of an armoured knight who lies canopied in a chancel wall recess. He is Sir Richard Goldsborough, who died in about 1333.

Sir Richard would doubtless know Sir Robert Plumpton, who, similarly armoured, lies in effigy in All Saints Church at Spofforth, south-east of Goldsborough. But more interesting to me and most of us is a humbler, yet surely, a more remarkable man whose tombstone may be found and read in the churchyard – John Metcalf, more famous as Blind Jack of Knaresborough. The triumph of the great roadmaker over his sightlessness seems to sing from the spirited rhythms of his forgotten biographer-poet –

Here lies John Metcalf; one whose infant sight
Felt the dark pressure of an endless night;
Yet such the fervour of his dauntless mind,
His limbs full strung, his spirit unconfin'd
That long ere yet life's bolder years began,
His sightless efforts marked th' aspiring man.
Nor mark'd in vain. High deede his manhood dar'd,
And commerce, travel, both his ardour shar'd;
'Twas his a guide's unerring aid to lend;
O'er trackless wastes to bid new roads extend;
And when Rebellion reared her giant size,
'Twas his to burn with patriot enterprise,
For parting wife and babes one pang to feel,
Then welcome danger for his country's weal.

Reader! like him exert thy utmost talent giv'n;
Reader! like him adore the bounteous Hand of Heav'n!

But more of Blind Jack when we reach Knaresborough, his birth-place.

Spofforth has the remains of a castle where Harry Hotspur, no less, was born. He died in battle, as did many others of his clan, and their chequered family fortunes are reflected in the story of the castle. It was burned by the victorious Yorkists after the battle of Towton in 1461, for, like so many ancient Yorkshire families, the Percys supported the Lancastrian cause.

One wall of Spofforth Castle's undercroft is formed by the living rock, which seems to suggest that the structure almost grew from the fabric of the earth itself. Of the whole castle, only about a third still stands, a morality in stone on the fate of those who live by conquest? Gamelbar, the original owner, who was dispossessed after the Conquest may be forgiven a ghostly chuckle as he contemplates the fortunes of his usurpers: 1403, Henry Hotspur killed at Shrewsbury; 1408, Henry Percy, first Earl of Northumberland, killed at Bramham Moor; 1461, the third earl and his brother killed at Towton; 1489, after the family had restored their fortunes, the heir to them killed by a mob in his manor at Topcliffe.

Restored yet again and lived in from time to time in the sixteenth century, the castle suffered final defeat in the Civil War. Yet the name of Percy is inextricably entwined in the story of Yorkshire, and, indeed, of England itself. There is a tradition, even, that Spofforth, too, may be almost as seminal a name in English constitutional history as Runny-mede; for it has been said that rebel barons met here in 1215 to hammer out the terms of the Magna Carta. True or false, the signature of

Richard de Percy was one of the first to be appended to the great charter of English liberty.

Just a few miles north-west of here, Rudding Park, set in sumptuous parkland and rose gardens, recalls Regency days – so much more gracious (at least on the surface) than the tumultuous times of the Percys. And older than either Rudding Park or Spofforth Castle are the millstone enormities of Plumpton Rocks.

It is impossible to think of Knaresborough – for me, at any rate – without remembering Mother Shipton – *and* Eugene Aram *and* Blind Jack Metcalf, three factual characters, whose true place appears almost to be in fiction – just as Knaresborough itself might seem to be more at home in a fairy story than in sober fact.

For anyone brought up in the West Riding, Knaresborough never quite loses its air of fantasy. Its Dropping Well alone widens juvenile eyes to the fullest extent as they contemplate a bewildering collection of objects – hats, gloves, toys and who knows what else – 'petrified' by the calcium in the water which has streamed down on them after pouring over a limestone rock.

Nearby is a cave in whose darkest corner you may discover (if your courage fail not) a hideous hag who stares at you with malevolent eyes. Don't be too alarmed – Mother Shipton, whose birthplace this cave purports to be, is here in effigy only, though you will find another representation of her close by. For the sign of the Mother Shipton Inn bears a picture of her, together with her supposed declaration:

> *Near this Petrifying Well*
> *I first drew breath, as records tell.*

There are, of course, those who say she never drew breath at all – there always are – but my belief in her is almost as strong as in Aram or Metcalf – though not in some of the prophecies which have been the chief reason for her fame!

However, it was not Mother Shipton, but one Charles Hindley, of Brighton, who made some of her most famous 'prophecies' (and published them in 1862) – such forecasts as the famous rhymes 'foretelling' the discovery of America, submarine and balloon travel, the Crystal Palace and the Crimean War.

> *Under water men shall walk,*
> *Shall ride, shall sleep and talk;*
> *In the air men shall be seen,*
> *In white, in black and in green.*

Mr Hindley eventually confessed to his deception, and that, you might have thought, would have been the end of the Knaresborough soothsayer. It was not: Mother Shipton is possibly better known today than she ever was and her legend provides Knaresborough with a miniature industry supported by the thousands who every year visit 'her' cave and buy mementoes of her career, real or imagined, and booklets telling the story of her life.

Mother Shipton, born Ursula Southeil in 1488 (or 1486, or 1581), was not only incredibly ugly, according to tradition, but her nose, 'of improportionable length . . . adorned with great pimples . . . gave strong lustre in the night!' So much so, in fact, that her foster-mother had no need of candles. Despite her ugliness, she took the fancy of one Toby Shipton, who came from Shipton near York, and they were married. Some say she had more to do with York than Knaresborough and perhaps she had, but she surely belongs in spirit to the Nidderdale town which has so taken her to its heart.

In a grimmer sense Eugene Aram seems suited to his niche in Knaresborough, though he, too, went to York – if only to be hanged there for the murder of Daniel Clark, whose bones were discovered in 1758 – many years after his mysterious disappearance.

Aram was born at Ramsgill in Upper Nidderdale in 1704. Already a brilliant scholar, he became the village schoolmaster, and the cottage where he taught school may still be seen there. He married Anna Spence, of Lofthouse, just up the dale, and that, perhaps, was his greatest mistake, for they were an ill-assorted pair.

Four years after his marriage, in 1734, he was appointed steward of a Knaresborough estate and it was in Knaresborough that he met Daniel Clark and the landlord of the Barrel Inn, Henry Terry. When Clark disappeared, having obtained a large quantity of goods on credit after coming into money, suspicion fell on Aram and Terry and a man called Houseman with whom Clark had been last seen. Some of Clark's goods were found in Aram's garden, but in spite of such incriminating discoveries, Aram was not prosecuted then, and he soon left Knaresborough and Anna for the South. It was there that he was apprehended, when, 14 years later, a labourer digging for limestone on Thistle Hill discovered a skeleton.

In fact, these were not the bones of Clark, but local rumour-mongers supposed they were. At the inquest Anna Spence told a damning tale about Eugene's and Houseman's suspicious behaviour on the night of Clark's disappearance. She may well have been motivated largely by hatred of the husband who had left her so many years before, but it was enough.

Houseman, committed to York Castle, accused Aram, though he said that Clark was buried not on Thistle Hill but in an ancient riverside hermitage, St Robert's Cave, which may be seen at Knaresborough to this day. Aram denied the charge, accusing Houseman and Terry, but he was found guilty and hanged at York, from where his body was taken to hang in chains at Knaresborough. The question of his guilt is still debated, perhaps because his tragedy seems all the greater for the undoubted brilliance demonstrated in his linguistic researches.

John Metcalf doubtless knew all about Aram, for they were contemporaries, though Metcalf was a dozen years younger than the schoolmaster. When he listened, avidly, as a man of about 40 to news of the gruesome discovery at Thistle Hill, Blind Jack, as he was now known, was on the threshold of the most successful phase of his amazing career.

When he caught smallpox as a young child his parents hardly expected him to survive; and when he was left blind before he was six years old they must have thought they would have a helpless beggar on their hands for the rest of their lives.

How wrong they were – for within a few years Jack had embarked on a career which included guiding travellers through the Forest of Knaresborough, fiddling for dancers in the inns at Harrogate and serving in the army as a sergeant's assistant during the Forty-five Rebellion. He eloped with his bride the night before her wedding, under the nose of the man her parents wanted her to marry. Nothing, it seemed, that other men could do, was too difficult for Blind Jack.

His chief claim to fame, however, is as a roadmaker. He seemed to have an uncanny gift for making roads where others had found it impossible. Altogether he built 180 miles of road, as well as a number of bridges, before dying in his ninety-third year at Spofforth, where, as we have seen, his tombstone still stands, inscribed with Jack's remarkable biography.

How did Jack perform his amazing feats? In Knaresborough Castle you may see at least two of the instruments he used – his stick and the 'waywiser' or 'viameter' by means of which he measured the land he walked over, totting up distances and assessing the difficulties of the terrain – difficulties, one might add, which for him existed only to be overcome. The stick, with its crooked top, is, I believe, only half its original length – so it is no use handling it as a walking stick in the hope of estimating Jack's height, which has been variously assessed at anything between six feet and seven-foot-three. This stick, if I mistake not, is all that remains of the one you may see in early woodcuts, and however tall Jack may have been, his staff was obviously taller still.

Some say Jack invented the 'viameter' or 'waywiser', but it was probably already in use before he took to roadmaking. Basically it was an iron-tyred wheel which Jack pushed before him, keeping a finger on the dial just below the handle, wherein was a pointer whose revolutions told him how far he had travelled between one point and the next.

At first sight, so little seems to remain of Knaresborough Castle that it might be considered hardly worth exploring – like a great, broken tooth, the rectangular keep is all that remains above ground of the fourteenth-century Royalist stronghold 'slighted' by Cromwell in 1648.

He may have watched its partial demolition with a heavy-hearted satisfaction, for it was outside these stubborn walls, four years before, that his own son was killed. Bordered on three sides by the Nidd and on the other by a 30-foot wall, it had defied its Roundhead besiegers (led by the great 'Black Tom' Fairfax) until supplies ran out. And then (Fairfax being his recognisable, chivalrous self) the defenders were allowed to march out with full military honours.

With such brave memories, the old place might feel just a little humiliated by the surrounding putting greens and smooth shaven lawns and seats where the grateful elderly may enjoy prospects of the Nidd.

The first stronghold was raised here in Saxon times. Later, after the murder of Thomas à Becket in 1170, four knights, including Hugh de Moreville, the castle's constable, hid here from the anger of the hasty king who had demanded to be rid of his turbulent priest. And the common folk of Knaresborough used to say that even the dogs would not eat the crumbs that fell from the table of such evil men.

Two centuries and more later, Richard II was a prisoner here. His quarters, known today as the King's Chamber, were no doubt pleasanter than the grim dungeon in whose walls traces of iron staples bear witness to past miseries of lowlier prisoners.

Knaresborough is more sophisticated today than I have ever known it – yet it clings to its past even more tightly. On the waterside recently I found a very smart-looking Italian restaurant, but guess what was on the roof – a balk of timber which is, we are assured, the original gibbet on which Eugene Aram was hanged. (All of which prompts the irreverent thought that murderers possibly do more to further the prosperity of the town which have known them than some blamelessly worthy alderman could claim.)

Granted, the town has other claims to fame. First of all – its setting, with red-roofed houses climbing the limestone cliff that overlooks the Nidd, as if this were some fishing village instead of an inland town. And had it no such colourful characters as the trio just mentioned, (and other oddities I have yet to describe) I would still enjoy a never-fading pleasure in merely walking along its river bank and wondering how on earth the builders contrived to insert houses and shops between the river and the beetling cliffs; and there would still be boatmen, inviting us to enjoy 'one mile of beautiful scenery in comfort', and thatched houses, and cobbled paths to climb.

Knaresborough is an ancient town. It was granted to one of the Conqueror's henchmen, called Serlo de Burgh, whose grandson, Eustace Fitz-John, built the castle, which is almost mundane compared to some of Knaresborough's curiosities. Where else would you find in one town Mother Shipton's Cave; *and* the Dropping Well *and* St Robert's Cave on the riverside, with its grim associations with Eugene Aram, not to mention Fort Montague – not at all what its name suggests, but a three-storey house hewn out of the solid rock of the cliff face. A weaver started the work, which was still unfinished after 16 years and so was left for his son to complete. While the excavation was in progress, the site had a distinguished visitor, the Duchess of Buccleuch, whose family name, Montague, was bestowed on the house in her honour. Whereupon the weaver, a Mr Hill, conferred upon himself the title 'Governor' of his fort. You go upstairs to the kitchen and down to the bedroom. (A true Knaresborough touch.)

To the right of the house is the Chapel of our Lady of the Crag, another excavation in the cliff. Often called St Robert's Chapel, it is no doubt sometimes confused with St Robert's Cave, now a Roman Catholic riverside shrine where mass has been celebrated from time to time.

A monk of Fountains Abbey and the son of a Mayor of York, St Robert was born in 1160 and died in 1218, whereupon the people of Knaresborough, who venerated him greatly, are said to have refused to allow his body to be removed from the town for burial at the Abbey. His bones are believed to rest near the altar in the chapel, though that was not excavated until about 1408 under a licence from Henry IV. Perhaps during the intervening 200 years they rested in the cave of which he had become so well-loved a tenant.

The chapel-shrine faithfully maintains the Knaresborough standard by being one of a very rare medieval type unique in England. And by the way, the larger-than-life, roughly carved 'crusader' in armour, about to draw his sword beside the chapel door, does not represent St Robert, and in fact probably began his 'sentry duty' as late as the eighteenth century.

Compared with such a rarity, Knaresborough's claim to possess 'the Oldest Chemist's Shoppe in England' seems almost commonplace.

Doubtless to its annoyance, Knaresborough now forms part of the enlarged Harrogate, itself in its way one of the most successful towns in Yorkshire. England's first 'watering place', as it claims to be, it was dispensing health (or so its visitors hoped) as early as the days of Charles II – golden days they certainly were for Harrogate, which has never really 'looked back' since the day in 1576 when William Slingsby discovered the first chalybeate spring at the hamlet of *Haywragate*, as it used to be called – the name probably meaning nothing more than 'the road passing near the park' (no doubt an enclosed portion of the Forest of Knaresborough).

Harrogate today, despite its pride in its 'bracing air', would hardly claim to be so effective medically as it did in the eighteenth century, when its sulphur well could apparently be visited in confident hope by sufferers from scrofula and worms, while the ancient Tewit Well offered relief in cases of the gravel.

The Tewit Well (Tewit being a version of pewit or lapwing) stands surmounted by a miniature stone 'temple' on Harrogate's justly and zealously prized park-like common, the Stray (which covers 215 acres and has a Spa Protection Society dedicated to its eternal preservation, along with the rights of 'ingress and egress' of Harrogate folk).

Today there are said to be 88 wells, many of them in the Valley Gardens but you will see none of the priestesses who once ministered at this temple of health. One such was Betty Lupton 'Queen of the Harrogate Wells', a formidable figure with the scoop and beaker she used to dispense sulphur water to the visitors whose money laid the foundations of Harrogate's fortunes. Was it Yorkshire's Victorian hypochondriacs, fat from the industrial sweat of the masses in Bradford, Huddersfield, Leeds and Halifax, who chiefly built upon those found-ations? Anyway, few towns have changed their purpose more – their form less – than Harrogate.

In the dear, dead days, chapel choirs from industrial areas would descend on Harrogate for their annual trips, delightfully conscious of shocking the superior place as they walked arm-in-arm along the sedate streets singing catchy choruses from their latest concerts. On just such an excursion one small boy asked for a bottle of 'pop' at a vaguely remembered floral hall refreshment bar, only to be met by an incomprehension which aroused even greater incredulity – what sort of a place was this, where they had never heard of pop?

Harrogate in those early 'thirties days was already in a state of transition, but hardly knew it. Bath chairs still abounded. The Royal Baths offered 'massage-douche, herthe vapour, liver pack with needle or shower', not forgetting what sounds a most formidable local speciality – the Harrogate carbonic acid bath!

And the baths, opened in 1897, dispensed health via the tap and the tub until 1969. You can still get a sauna or a Turkish bath there but at the slightest risk, perhaps, of feeling rather anachronistic – while all around are listening to concerts or watching fashion or film shows, or looking at exhibitions of pictures, for which events the Baths now provide a setting.

Something of the old Harrogate atmosphere survives here in the former Pump Room, but instead of squaring your shoulders as you approach a dispenser in the middle of the room, and demanding a glass of something so revolting that it could only do you incalculable good, today you sit at a table and sip coffee to the accompaniment of an urbane pianist who is no more likely to shock your ears with anything too *avant garde* than he is to lapse into rock 'n' roll.

You may, of course, be ill or reckless enough to insist on taking the waters – in which case you will be directed to the Pump Room Museum there to sample (among other appropriate relics of old Harrogate) what has been likened to rotten eggs beaten up in paraffin.

This museum is an exhibit in itself – a good example of Harrogate's adaptability. It is an attractive, domed, octagonal building dating from 1842, the year the original covering of the well here was taken away to cover the Tewit Well. Other wells, which have kept their houses but changed their way of life, are now boutiques, sweet shops, ice-cream kiosks and even (ingloriously perhaps) a gardener's hut.

Queen Victoria, I feel, if she were suddenly to arrive in Harrogate, would find little at first to shock her – except, of course, the traffic. And even if that disturbed her, she would be reassured when she spotted her statue at the North Eastern Hotel and her name on Victoria Avenue, together with such other evidence of Harrogate's loyalty as Prince of Wales Mansions and Windsor House (formerly the Grand Hotel).

She would surely approve of the renaming of the 'Kursaal' as the Royal Hall. Today (like the Royal Baths) the Royal Hall is a setting for conferences and in such transformation lies the explanation of the town's wonderfully successful adaptation to a changing way of life. As the health-seekers dwindled, the enormous hotels, too, found a new purpose as Harrogate began to grow into a leading conference, trade fair and exhibition centre.

Toy fairs, fancy goods fairs, pet fairs. Rarely (perhaps never) a week passes without some remarkable event which *would* surprise Queen Victoria!

Harrogate, once the floral health resort, is now the floral conference centre – still with its hotels and flower beds; still, even, with its wells and their 'waters': recently a Yorkshire company began bottling Harrogate spring water. The Victorian aspect is strengthened by the abundance of churches – St Peter's in the town centre; the magnificent St Wilfrid's, begun by Temple Moore, who built the nave and chancel between 1905 and 1914, and finished 20 years later by Leslie Moore, his nephew, who designed the transepts and the Lady Chapel. The faces of characters in frescoes showing scenes from the life of Christ are those which were once to be seen in the congregation.

Harrogate, perhaps uniquely, combines earnestness of purpose with a continental gaiety exemplified by its French Weeks and waiters' races.

Its annual festival attracts leading exponents from all over the world. And, being a Yorkshire festival, I believe it even makes money. Harrogate is an ideal centre for Dales visitors, but we must not linger here too long. But do stay long enough – architecture, shops, the Harlow Car Gardens of the Northern Horticultural Society, the Great Yorkshire Show every July . . . Harrogate truly has everything. I dare say it's safe even to ask for a bottle of pop there, nowadays.

We meet the 'continental' note again four miles north of Harrogate on the Ripon road – at Ripley, where the small castle of the Ingilbys (who still live there) reigns over a 'typical French village'. It was Sir William Amcotts Ingilby who remodelled the place in 1827 on the lines of a village in Alsace Lorraine. Thus, the village hall is inscribed 'Hotel de Ville'.

After the Battle of Marston Moor, Cromwell inflicted his unwelcome presence as guest of the Royalist Ingilbys. The story has been often told before, but I cannot help recalling the scene as Oliver spent an uneasy night on a sofa, whilst across the hall his unwilling hostess, Lady Ingilby sat, watching him closely, two pistols in her apron! Next morning he rode away, leaving behind an invincible woman who grudgingly admitted that he had behaved peaceably enough – but added that if he hadn't he'd never have left the house alive.

His would have been one more death to add to the unnumbered casualties of the battle fought 15 miles east of here – and not all of the dead were killed in battle. In the wall of Ripley church I was shown the marks made by bullets fired at Royalist prisoners lined up against the east wall. What had they done to perish so miserably? Why the apparent absence of chivalry in a war so often chivalrous?

When the Roundhead troops were billeted there, the village had yet to be 'Frenchified'; the castle was still to be rebuilt (in 1780); but the church, which dates mostly from 1400, though the clerestory and upper tower were built in 1567, was much as it is today. And in the churchyard would be at least the base of the mysterious medieval weeping cross we can see there today. It has eight niches where penitents could kneel – that much we know, but its exact purpose is far from clear. Perhaps when Cromwell visited the church the cross was complete. Could it be that he himself ordered its decapitation as a symbol of popery? He was certainly scandalised by the magnificence of the Ingilby tombs within the church, and must have glowered as he read a glowing tribute to 'Sir William Inglebie', before curtly ordering the addition of the words: 'No pompe nor pride. Let God be honoured'.

But what a tale Lady Ingilby would have to tell Sir William when he returned from battle with his sister, 'Trooper Jane', who dressed like a soldier and rode with the troop of horse raised by the Ingilby family!

Hampsthwaite, a mile or two south-west of Ripley was important in Roman times because of the river crossing here. Today it is one of my best-loved Nidderdale villages – not because it has any great claims to beauty (may its inhabitants forgive me) but because of its ghosts – or at least, the three that I know of. Two of them surely haunt the Church of St Thomas à Becket there. Not in the traditional, spectral sense – they are much too restful for that. Or at least one of them is, to judge by her serene effigy. I refer to Amy Woodforde-Finden, composer of the Indian Love Lyrics. The other members of this remarkably varied trio are a local character surnamed Barker, whose great skill belied his nickname, 'Blind Peter', and William Makepeace Thackeray no less.

But it is the shade of the lady composer with an eastern aura that makes the most striking impact in this rather sober village of Lower Nidderdale. If the white marble effigy reclining on her tomb is really the speaking likeness it is said to be, she was as beautiful as her life was tragic. She was born in Valparaiso, where her father, Alfred Ward, was British consul. Her invalid stepson, Eric, lived in Hampsthwaite for some time in the care of the local doctor. When he died in 1913 he was buried in the churchyard. Only three years later his father joined him there and in 1919 the family was united in death by the death of the composer herself.

The white marble Amy has the company of cherubs on her journey through eternity and, lest the years should erase her fame, scenes from her best-loved compositions are carved on the base of her sepulchre. The Jhelum River of Kashmir, the domes and minarets of a mosque, desert palms and lush paddy fields all recall almost forgotten favourites like 'Pale Hands I loved Beside the Shalimar' or 'Far Across the Desert Sands'. White irises, too, associated with Kashmiri funeral rites, are carved at each side of the tomb.

Blind Peter's memorials are less explicit, and there is considerable mystery about one of them (quite near the composer's tomb), a painting of a man, said to have been made by the daughter of a former vicar of Hampsthwaite.

Probably the figure shown leaning on a large font does represent Blind Peter, but as far as I know, there is no proof of that. There is little doubt, however, that the wooden clock-face nearby is all that now remains of a clock Peter restored to active life and lovingly maintained.

His tombstone recalls that 'though blind from infancy he was skilful as a cabinet maker, a glazier and a musician'. He was born in 1808 and lost his sight at the age of four (when he was two years younger than John Metcalf, of Knaresborough, though in Peter's case the reason was 'inflammation of the eyes', not smallpox). Like Jack, Peter quickly became as skilful as any sighted boy at climbing trees, fishing and haymaking. And, again like Metcalf, he became a popular fiddler at dances and feasts. He also taught himself to use the tools belonging to a deaf and dumb cabinet-maker friend. I wonder how they conversed.

Blind Peter's furniture was stoutly made and well finished. One of his descendants, a retired schoolteacher, once showed me an extending table he had made. Here and there in this part of Nidderdale there are said to be other solid, apparently indestructible pieces of furniture made by this remarkable man.

Peter Barker may never have seen his wife but he married her twice – within a fortnight! The first wedding took place in a register office, much to the displeasure of the then vicar of Hampsthwaite. To satisfy him, a second ceremony was held in church, and no doubt the Reverend Mr Shann felt that his blessings had been efficacious when Peter took his baby son to church to be christened. Sadly, he had lost both wife and son when the boy was only 17, but found comfort by reading in his cottage from a Bible with embossed letters, and playing the violin he had made.

Despite his loss, he eventually regained his cheerful disposition. He loved to tell visitors the story of the clock he had revived when it apparently went on strike (or rather, refused to strike) in protest at the treatment it had received at the hands of a seaman, who would give it a 'feather-full' of oil once a year, presumably between voyages. Without a clock the folk of Hampsthwaite had no means of knowing when to rise and when to retire for the night, which to Peter seemed all wrong! He knew nothing of clock-making, but that did not deter him. Feeling about inside it, he soon discovered the secrets of the clock's mechanism, and great was the delight of the vicar when the old clock, whose 'ailment' had defied so many 'experts', struck again. Ten shillings a year the church-wardens paid Peter for looking after the clock whose face alone now remains to remind us of him.

Thackeray, though the most eminent of the trio, is the least mysterious. The graves of his family, like the bones of Blind Peter and of the husband and stepson of Amy Woodforde-Finden, lie among the ancient graves in the neat burial ground of the church (surely one of the best things about Hampsthwaite). There is also a tiny cottage where he is said to have stayed, perhaps while revisiting old haunts. What a pity the author of *Vanity Fair*, whose family had lived for generations at Hampsthwaite, cannot be added to the list of towering Yorkshire writers, but he was born far away from Hampsthwaite – in Calcutta.

Did I mention *three* Hampsthwaite ghosts? There is, perhaps, a fourth, but since Jane Ridsdale, whose memorial is in the church's south aisle, was only 31 inches tall when she died aged 59, I hope to be forgiven for overlooking her.

The Nidd winds between Burnt Yates and Birstwith. The name of the

former may well have started out as Bond Gates, meaning the boundary
gates or monk wall marking off Fountains Abbey property from the
Forest of Knaresborough. Birstwith is notable for the Victorian
Swarcliffe Hall which stands on the site of a house where poor Charlotte
Brontë came on holiday as governess with the unspeakable Sidgwick
children from Stonegappe in Lothersdale. That must have been even
worse than being at home with them. Dacre Banks, long loved by Youth
Hostellers, was the setting for a grange belonging to Fountains Abbey,
who held mining rights here.

If there had been no schoolchildren taking their first cautious steps in
rock-climbing on my last visit to Brimham Rocks, I might have
underestimated their hugeness, even though I had seen them often
enough before. Until you are standing close beneath their convoluted
statuary they appear dwarfed by their setting – 1,000 feet above sea level
in a great natural 'park' of 60 acres with views over a Yorkshire
panorama covering 36 miles and taking in, on a clear day, Knaresborough Castle and York Minster.

These rocks – dozens of them – are grotesquely, fascinatingly
beautiful. They have been a tourist attraction for over 200 years, and the
work done recently at the site by the National Trust, aided by the
Countryside Commission, will ensure that their attraction in the future
is even greater.

Unquestionably a great part of their appeal has been their magnificent setting among the moorland heights of Nidderdale; and the
vegetation which grows between, around and on the rocks themselves. It
was being destroyed through Brimham's very popularity, but now,
through the provision of discreetly sited car parks and other amenities,
including an information centre in Brimham House, a formerly derelict
shooting lodge, the rocks will become increasingly beautiful as nature
reclaims her own.

It seems belittling, somehow, to attach trivial and transitory names
such as Flowerpot, Gorilla, Sphinx and Oyster to these huge masses of
millstone grit. The rocks will have visitors for centuries to come, and
some of them are sure to ask 'Who *was* General de Gaulle?' (even if they
have no identification problem with 'Donald Duck'). By then, no doubt,
future ages will have formed their own names for the Druid's Coffin, the
Cannon, the Yoke of Oxen and the Dancing Bear, which already have a
dated ring. At least such names as the Druid's Writing Desk, Druid's
Castle and the Idol give a clue to the rather wild surmises of eighteenth-
century visitors. For the late eighteenth and early nineteenth centuries
were only too partial to Druids, especially when theorising about the
origins of Brimham Rocks.

Such fancies were given a helpful boost by a certain Major Rooke,
who, after his visit to the Rocks, informed the Antiquarian Society of his

conviction that they could only have been the creation of 'artists skilled in the power of mathematics'. The rocks soon became known as 'Druidical monuments'. They are not, of course, but never mind: the truth is more awe-inspiring even than the Druids.

Brimham's story begins 300,000,000 years ago in a Britain almost equatorial. Scotland and Norway were linked then by a mountain range from which rivers washed down the sand and mud which was to form the millstone grit of Nidderdale. For century after century those rivers ran, until the grit delta here was 5,000 feet thick. As layer was laid upon layer, the grit became increasingly hard and compacted, bound together by a natural cement into a resistant sandstone, fissured with long vertical cracks.

The unhurried aeons of geological time saw this hard, fissured sandstone overlaid by other rocks of later systems, only to surface again during a long, slow upheaval affecting the whole of England. And as the earth's surface heaved slowly upward, the softer upper rocks were worn away, and now the gritstone was once more near the top. If rocks had eyes they would have seen a Britain hard to recognise as the tropical land which formed them – a country locked in endless, ever-deepening winter until all was frozen and ice reigned supreme.

But only change is permanent. Slowly, slowly the ice melted first from the hills – though still the valleys were glacier-bound and still the cold was intense as wind and rain and frost assailed the rocks exposed at the sides of the hills, eating into and enlarging the cracks, breaking pieces away to be washed down the hillside as fragments and pebbles. And during the thousands of years that followed, wind and rain continued the grotesque sculpture with a slowness inconceivable by our minds, reducing everything to its elements to be reformed again and again in Nature's endless flux.

Inevitably the great rocks have attracted legends, like that of two star-crossed lovers Edwin and Julia, who fled from unsympathetic parents to be overtaken at Brimham Rocks, whereupon they scrambled to the top of a crag now called the Lovers' Rock, joined hands and prepared to jump to their deaths.

And jump they did, but as so often happens in such tales they were miraculously saved – by the fairies, by the girl's crinoline serving as a parachute or whatever you wish. Naturally, the hard-hearted parents relented after this rather melodramatic exhibition. No doubt they were a little anxious as to what the lovers might try next! So everything ended happily – as far as we know. . . .

Much less romantic is the legend attached to the Rocking Stone which moves easily – provided it's an honest man who pushes it. Surely a Lancastrian fabricated the story that it has yet to move for a Yorkshireman.

By way of Low Laithe and Wilsill, passing Smelthouses to our right, we approach Pateley Bridge – rather a let-down if I may be so rude! But in fairness, few towns could appear as a vision of loveliness after you'd reached them via such delightsome routes – whichever way you get there.

And Pateley, after all, was not built to be an urban showpiece. Yet if it lacks beauty it compensates for that in interest. It has been a market town since the fourteenth century and cattle and sheep are still sold there; but 'Badgers' Field' (which is what the name means) underwent a drastic change in the nineteenth century when the North Eastern Railway opened a branch line from Harrogate, boosting the fortunes of this place, where for centuries stone had been quarried, lead and iron mined. Now, by train-loads, the visitors came to 'Little Switzerland', as it claimed to be, making it the tourist centre it has remained.

The great reservoir schemes further opened up Nidderdale – disastrously, some would say. In furtherance of these, in 1907 Britain's first municipally owned passenger railway – the Nidd Valley Light Railway – was built from Pateley to Lofthouse, with stations at Wath and Ramsgill. Though the tracks were taken up in 1936 after rusting in idleness for seven years when motor bus services had rendered them superfluous, the course of the line can still be traced and some at least of the station buildings remain.

In Pateley Bridge Museum (housed in what was once the workhouse) you may learn much about the making of the great artificial lakes which mark the Nidd's early course. In this very building, apparently, workers engaged on making Scar House Reservoir were billeted until a village to house them was created in the wild wastelands high up the dale. Daily they travelled to their work by train until the great job was finished and the village, no longer needed, was demolished. A faded cutting from the *Daily Mail* records the last events under the headlines

> Village is sold and a railway too
> Nod your head and buy an engine.

The 357 lots at that sale must have made Scar House resemble a giant's toyshop, with steam engines, cranes and locomotives, all seen as bargains, no doubt, by the 250 dealers, engineers, colliery owners, metal refiners and scrap merchants who came to buy. There will be more to say of this vast undertaking when we reach what still remains of it. But before leaving dear old Patley, with its tunnel-like main street made all the darker by the colour of the local millstone grit, spare a thought for the rather unkindly named 'Yorke's Folly', one of two 'stoops' (once

9 Harewood House, designed by John Carr but with embellishments suggested by Robert Adam

10 *opposite*: Bolton Priory – 'a mixed museum of architectural styles representing the four centuries of the Priory's life'

11 *above*: Burnsall – the font in the church bears Norse symbols to match carved Viking tombstones

12 Hubberholme Church. Somehow its beautiful rood loft, carved in 1558, survived the Reformation

13 *opposite:* Harrogate – the 'watering place' that found a new purpose

14 *opposite:* Knaresborough Castle, once the hiding place for Thomas à Becket's murderers

15 *above:* Catrake Force, near Keld in Swaledale

16 Penhill, Wensleydale

there were three) erected by one of the Yorke family to provide work at a time when jobs were hard to get. Even if it hardly employed the near-thousand men who, years later, were to work on reservoir building, the project was none the less welcomed in its day.

From Pateley Bridge to Grassington a road climbs steeply to Greenhow, at 1,300 feet Yorkshire's highest village and surely one of the highest in England. Here they take a sombre pride in having some of the harshest winters in the country, but recall even savager winters when horses and carts were driven over the snow at wall-top height to gather peat, which provided the warmth essential to survival. Such privations are recalled during conversations in the Miners Arms, where, for a lark, miners once burnt the clothes of two braggarts among their number who had been encouraged to race naked for a mile in the snow – and found themselves locked out!

Greenhow Hill has been likened to a rotten cheese in which, since Roman times, men have burrowed like mice in search of lead. Latterly the spoil they cast aside as useless has been searched for fluorspar used by steel makers.

I have before me as I write 'Broadsheet No. 1' of the Greenhow Association, formed with the object of opposing any sort of large-scale mineral working which might, in their view, endanger health and safety on Greenhow, or destroy its traditional beauty and peace by surface quarrying or underground mining.

Slaves of the Romans – and even they were not the first – dug here for lead. A pig of Roman-inscribed lead from Greenhow found its way to the British Museum and another is said to be at Ripley Castle. In the 1860s a severe drop in lead prices almost killed the industry, and it struggled on until about 50 years ago, linked with an almost incredibly hard way of life that produced men of great hardihood and indomitable spirit. Their perseverance and enthusiasm had to be equal to the inevitable disappointments and constant hazards of their precarious craft. The quest for fluorspar recalled at least one miner to open a vein in a disused quarry and work there, like the miners of old with tools no more complicated than hammer and crowbar, pick and shovel; but used with a skill and knowledge born of long experience. More often a bulldozer did the donkeywork.

This is the country that is haunted by 'T'Owd Man', the archetypal lead miner whose spirit is the spectral summation of the many who lived and died extracting lead from these begrudging fells. And inevitably it was two miners – they surely wondered if the boggarts had bewitched them – who one day in 1860 blundered into Stump Cross Caverns. Today, on payment of a fee, we may see what met their astonished gaze, but in our case with the benefit of electric light, cunningly coloured to bring out the long-hidden beauty of the Fairy Fountain, the Cathedral, the Jewel Box, the Snow Drift, the Chamber of Pillars or, if you insist on being scientific, 'calcite formations' and stalactites.

Some day, perhaps, the psychical researchers will ascend Greenhow Hill and try to contact 't' Owd Man' himself – if the boggarts, who doubtless know him, do not drown them in the pothole pools or the witches put a spell on them first! Let the ghost-hunters be warned to do as the miners themselves did and wear a 'lucky stone' – if they can find one – around their necks. Strange things happen at Greenhow, especially when the moon is full: the sound of clogs has several times been heard crunching on the gravel of the road and sometimes, chillingly, *on the cobblestones close by* as the hearer stood at his own cottage door. Hard-headed surveyors, as well as down-to-earth local folk, have heard them – yet never a soul have they seen. . . .

Greenhow has one of the bleakest cemeteries I have ever seen, but it was the ghost of a man said to have been buried 50 yards *outside* its walls that for many years haunted the memories of the lead miners who troubled his slumber.

John Kaye was his name. He was a soldier who dropped dead after a forced march one hot day from Pateley Bridge. His grave was still pointed out years later but in the 1880s some lead-miners insisted it was nobbut a tale, and to explode it they dug at the spot – only to find that the story was true after all: there was a skeleton, some brass buttons and even a gun to prove it.

Imagine the miners' dread. Superstitious fears mixed with qualms of conscious made them rebury the remains, wondering silently how the spirit of John Kaye might revenge himself on those who had first doubted his existence and then disturbed his rest.

Anxious to appease the shade, they gave the grave a headstone and a footstone. Then, since directly beneath the grave there ran one of the mine workings, they carved into its roof the shape of a coffin. And thereafter, whenever a miner passed beneath the last lonely resting place of soldier Kaye, he would reach up, and out of fearful friendliness 'give him a knock'.

Considering they are both in Nidderdale, Wath, at the southern end of Gouthwaite Reservoir, could hardly be more unlike Greenhow. For Wath is as bland and restful as Greenhow is bleak and inseparable from toil and hardship. Wath, whose very name could hardly be softer, is a place to relax in before – or after – venturing on to Dallowgill Moor to the north, or meeting the 1,200-foot challenge of High Ruckles.

But my best-loved of all Nidderdale villages lies at the northern end of Gouthwaite's man-made lake (if this compensation reservoir on the site once occupied by a glacial lake can really be called man-made).

Enjoying an excellent dinner at the Yorke Arms at Ramsgill that night, I heard above the evening breeze the unhappy ghost of Eugene Aram moaning – as indeed he had good reason to do – while visiting the village of his earliest and probably happiest years.

I was shown the cottage where Eugene held his first school. He probably loathed Ramsgill and saw its inhabitants as clodhoppers. Yet he apparently loved his mother, if not his neighbours. In one cottage in Ramsgill, I am told, there is a portrait of that lady carved by Eugene himself in stone. Another relic of Aram, his travelling chest, lined with pages from the Bible, found its way to Ripley Castle, where his father was a gardener.

But, except in my imagination, the murderer of David Clark does not really haunt Ramsgill: the moans I had heard were merely the discordant cries of peacocks, one of which, next morning I found on the green displaying the full glory of his tail to an indifferent audience of several pea hens, a couple of lambs and their mother.

All this and peacocks, too! Was there no end to Ramsgill's riches? Even its name is right. It could possibly be more mellifluous but it is certainly born of the dale. For rams, ewes and their lambs, though inescapable in all the dales, seemed to be most noticeable around Ramsgill that spring, nibbling assiduously at the tender green leaves of the hawthorn that had appeared, it seemed, weeks late, and was all the more welcome for that.

It would be hard, I think, to improve on Ramsgill. Travelling up-dale you suddenly see the church tower, and almost before you know it you are in the village itself, where the long building of the Yorke Arms faces the green. On first acquaintance Nidderdale buildings of millstone grit look drab beside the silvery limestone of, say, Wharfedale, but Nidderdale's charm is no less persuasive for this sombreness, and nowhere more beguiling than in Ramsgill.

It is a small village centred around its green and cross, and some of its cottages have streamside gardens that almost dazzle you. In April, daffodils are everywhere. No one is surprised that Ramsgill has been adjudged Best Kept Village in the Lower Dales, but that seems faint praise: you feel it could hardly be other than well kept and that it demands a much higher commendation than a prosaic compliment on its state of preservation! And look at its surroundings. Footpaths and bridleways lead to tiny Bouthwaite and then to Wath, passing close to Gouthwaite's famous reservoir. A frolic of young lambs played King of the Castle over and over again on a pile of bales of hay. The air was filled with a bleating that mingled with the all-pervading sound of bird-song.

I kept my eyes upon the water as we walked, trying to identify the birds on and around its surface. Two miles long and a third of a mile in average width, it holds a staggering 1,564,000,000 gallons. Nearly 200 kinds of birds have been recorded here by the Harrogate Naturalists' Society – divers and grebes of several kinds – and the one which everyone hopes some day to see – a golden eagle.

Somewhere beneath all that water stood the old house of the Yorkes, whose folly we saw on Guyscliffe near Pateley Bridge and whose arms adorn the inn at Ramsgill.

Only a mile or two up the dale is Lofthouse, again quite unlike Ramsgill, with old houses dropped anyhow along the meandering main street that turns into a moorland road – and some less attractive modern ones – at least to my eyes – lower down on each side of the main road up the dale. Eastward lies Hambleton Hill – 1,331 feet.

Should I really be surprised by the advice on the war memorial fountain at Lofthouse. Advocating the liberal use of cold water 'inside and out', it is the work of a Dalesman-by-adoption who came from – of all places – Scotland. Certainly you could hardly be unaware of water hereabouts. A mile or so west of Lofthouse is How Stean Gorge, where the How Stean Beck courses between cliffs 70 feet deep. It has been called the Grand Canyon in miniature and though it is hardly that, it is certainly worth visiting.

For a small charge you may perambulate along rustic bridges which cross and recross the chasm; you may wander along fenced galleries carved in the cliff face over many years by the water. If you have wellingtons, wear them, for at times you will be walking over naked rock which can be wet and slippery. And if you're more than four foot nine and by some unlikely chance you have a tin hat in the car, that, too, could be useful, because in places the overarching rock roof is low.

Inevitably the Victorians called this, too, Little Switzerland. At least, those who had never seen Switzerland did. Who, I wonder, was Tom Taylor, who gave his name to the cave you can enter from here, where once a hoard of Roman coins were found? And who was Elgin after whom the nearby 'Hole', known for its stalagmites, is named?

From How Stean you can see Middlesmoor Church reigning over that windswept little village at the very head of the dale. You reach it by a road which attains a one-in-four gradient just before the Wesleyan chapel bids you a dour welcome to the cluster of cottages and farm buildings which, given a strong enough gust of wind, might easily topple down the hill . . . or so it seems.

In 1484, when Richard III was king, Archbishop Drummond of York rode through the Forest of Middlesmoor with a choir of men to consecrate the first church here, at the earnest request of villagers who had had enough of the long, lonely hazardous journey to Kirkby Malzeard in Wensleydale, whenever they needed the ministrations of their mother church.

In the north aisle is a treasured bell that might have been rung at that consecration. And here, too, are parts of a cross to St Chad, who is believed to have preached beside it when he was Bishop of Lichfield in 664. Inevitably we meet another of the Yorkes – Sir John. A brass plate informs us that he was Master of the Horse to Charles II – as well as M.P. for Richmond for all of 30 years.

The church is full of old acquaintances – and sometimes ghosts. For in the church register is recorded the marriage of *Eugenius Aram*, who in 1731 climbed this steep hill to make Anna Spence of Lofthouse his wife. In the following year their daughter, also Anna, was both baptised and buried.

I wonder if 'Eugenius' and Anna were too preoccupied with their newly married status to pause before setting off down that steep slope from the churchyard and look over the view – one of the finest in Yorkshire – that extends below Pateley Bridge. In their day, of course, there would be no Gouthwaite Reservoir – only the Nidd, like a twisting, flashing thread of silver between the high moorlands of Dallowgill and Heathfield.

This is pot-hole country, with vast caves like Goyden Pot and Manchester Hole, six hundred feet long, which swallows the Nidd – it emerges near Lofthouse. They are dangerous ('super severe', say the experts) – and also awe-inspiring – like Scar House Reservoir, the man-made marvel that is our destination. From here a track leads north to Deadman's Hill, where the bodies of three headless Scots pedlars, some say, were unearthed in 1728; while to the west, Little Whernside rises to almost 2,000 feet and to the south its bigger brother tops that figure by more than 300.

Work on Scar House, the bigger of Nidd's two 'great lakes', began when a square of this springy turf was cut on 5 October 1921. Three years later, on 17 July 1924, the construction work began and the reservoir was opened in September 1936. Six hundred yards long and 154 feet deep, at the maximum, it holds 2,000m. gallons to slake Bradford's thirst.

The vastness of the task of making it matched the immensity of its setting. On the dam's southern side they built a village with ten large hostels for workmen, and bungalows for staff, foremen, technicians. There was a school, a store, concert hall, cinema, church, a hospital with a doctor and a nurse in residence. Eight hundred men worked here when the labours were at their height and the village had a population of 1,250.

Today, where children laughed and played and neighbours shopped and chatted, the curlews cry over the grassy outlines that show where houses stood.

Begun in 1904, Angram, the first reservoir to trap the descending

Nidd, was finished in 1919, two years before Scar House was begun. In its giant fish-tail shape, 400 yards long, near the foot of Great Whernside, it holds over 1,000m. gallons.

FIVE

Wensleydale

Ripon to Lonely Lunds

Visit Ripon in August and you stand the best chance of seeing St Wilfrid. He had a great deal to do with this, Yorkshire's smallest city, and every August he returns to ride around on a white horse. You can recognise him by his long beard, his mitre and his crozier, for St Wilfrid was, of course, a bishop, and he founded Ripon Cathedral.

It is not, therefore, surprising that on the day of his feast, when his present-day proxy visits Ripon, representatives of its daily life accompany him in procession on his tour. And a light-hearted occasion it proves to be: I remember seeing the pantomime cow which was part of the Young Farmers' Club contingent being energetically shooed away by the Dean of the day as it tried to mount the cathedral steps.

Appointed Bishop of York in 669 Wilfrid found York Minster in a sad state of neglect and set about strengthening the walls and repairing and raising the roof. At Ripon, Eata, Abbot of Melrose, had founded a monastery, built of wood, in 657. It lasted only a few years, whereas the crypt of Wilfrid's church has lasted from about 670, when he succeeded Eata as abbot.

Few Christian structures in England are older than this little room – about 11 feet by eight and less than ten feet to the barrel roof's highest point – at the foot of 12 steps. What a contrast is such lowliness, with the majesty of Ripon's vault, at 90 feet one of the highest in England. Here is a relic of Saxon England, though Ripon's first Christian community had been founded by Scottish monks. I wonder if they resented the appointment of the Northumbrian Wilfrid as their Superior? If so, he doubtless knew how to deal with them, as he often did with kings and his fellow bishops. But he was not always successful in getting his own way, and when he fell out finally with the ruler of the time, he was deposed.

The millstone grit of which Ripon's minster church is built gives it a dour look, in keeping with the impression of strength conveyed especially to those who first see it from the front. But take a look inside those austere walls at the marvellous and far from austere wood carving by Ripon craftsmen who lived and worked perhaps five centuries ago.

In the nave of this cathedral Cromwell's troopers stabled their horses while taking Charles I to London – and his death. The King himself spent the night in the stable of a house since occupied by an aunt of Naomi Jacob, the novelist born in Ripon, whose grandfather kept an old posting house, the Unicorn Hotel . . . which brings me to Old Boots and a degree of light relief. . . .

As the *Wonderful Magazine* put it in 1793: 'This extraordinary man lived long at an inn (The Unicorn) at Ripon. By nature and habit he acquired the power of holding a piece of money between his nose and chin. His chief employment was waiting on the customers and from the circumstance of his cleaning their shoes and boots he went by the name of Old Boots'. The Unicorn still stands at Ripon, but alas, without Old Boots.

Few cities, anywhere, contain so much of interest in so small a space as Ripon. At its centre is the market square which Daniel Defoe called the most beautiful in England. From the centre of that rises a 90-foot obelisk erected in 1781 to honour the fact that William Aislabie of Studley Royal had been Ripon's M.P. for 60 years. Visit the square at nine in the evening and you will see a ceremony which has been performed here since the days of Alfred the Great: a man wearing a tricorn hat and carrying a great curved horn enters the square and sounds the horn once at each corner and once in front of the mayor's house. He is 'setting the watch', a custom which began when, instead of a mayor, Ripon had a 'Wakeman', who for a fee of twopence per door per year insured the citizens against their houses being robbed between the setting of the watch and sunrise.

There is no Wakeman today, but the thirteenth-century Wakeman's House, now a museum, still looks out on the square and his office of mayor-cum-constable is recalled in the city's motto: 'Except the Lord keep the city the Wakeman waketh in vain'.

At Ripon's Thursday market, the Corn Bell is rung to announce that trading can now begin. It has in fact been going on for hours. That custom dates from the time when the Archbishop of York could exact a corn tax of two handfuls from each sack – *if* his tax man could get to the market before the farmers had done their business and decamped!

South-east of Ripon is Boroughbridge with its mysterious 'Devil's Arrows', three gritstone monoliths from the Bronze Age, 18 to 22 feet high, standing in a direct line. Once there were seven, but a farmer I met trying to manoeuvre his tractor around the 'arrow' in his field made it clear that he had quite enough with one!

One day, in a grumpy mood, the devil issued the warning:

> *Boro 'brigg stand out o' t way*
> *For Aldborough town I will ding down*

Fortunately, he was no better a marksman than he was a poet and in spite of his arrows, Aldborough still remains, as it has since it was Isurium Brigantum, a Roman settlement, headquarters of the Ninth Legion. Here are the foundations of a complete Roman town and, among many other remains, a fine tesselated pavement.

Much more recent are the antiquities at Newby Hall, at Skelton, west of Boroughbridge, where the late Queen Mary on a visit in 1936 was much intrigued by a unique collection (as she herself called it) of chamber pots from all over Europe and the Far East. They range from rough peasant ware of the sixteenth century to the finest china, and bear some surprising inscriptions!

The gardens of the Hall, a Queen Anne house, step gracefully down to the Ure – and wonderful they are. They were the creation, over many years, of Major Edward Compton with whom I once had the privilege of a guided tour of the grounds. I doubt if there are more beautiful gardens in England.

The seventeenth-century diarist Celia Fiennes called it 'the finest house I saw in Yorkshire' and she had seen many. The main block of the present house was built by Sir Edward Blackett, M.P. for Ripon in 1689, in the style of Wren. After Sir Edward's death the house was acquired by the collector and connoisseur William Weddell, who hired Robert Adam to extend and redesign it.

Weddell had a famous collection of classical sculpture and it was chiefly to house this that Adam added a wing on the left of the east front, balanced by an identical wing on the right. To house Weddell's Gobelin tapestries Adam created the tapestry room which some consider his finest work at Newby Hall. The tapestries, one of only five sets in existence, represent the Amours of the Gods.

An ancestor of the family now living at Newby was Sir Robert Vyner, goldsmith to Charles II, who commissioned him to remake the royal regalia, (destroyed by Cromwell) in preparation for his coronation. The fee for the work was never paid and though Sir Robert (who was also the royal banker) was granted an annuity, he died the king's creditor to the tune of £416,000. The family still have the royal I.O.U.

The Vyner family history abounds in such surprising and colourful details – not least those of violent or tragic deaths. Clare Vyner, for instance, died as a result of the capsizing of a ferry carrying horses and huntsmen across the Ure, and Frederick Vyner was murdered in 1870 by Turkish brigands in Greece. Money paid as compensation by the Greek Government was spent in building the Church of Christ the Consoler, near the gates of Newby Park.

A book could easily be written on Newby Hall: and even more stories might be told of an ancient house to the south-west of Newby. But Markenfield Hall seems to enclose its long history in reticence as the house itself is encircled by a moat. One of the oldest of inhabited houses, it represents an earlier, more perilous age, which was reflected in the lives of the Markenfields themselves. Though John de Markenfield crenellated his mansion in 1311 (in days when an Englishman's home *had* to be his castle), a descendant, Sir Thomas, proved 250 years later, that castles could be lost. He lost his in the Rising of the North, which cost other Yorkshire Catholics their lands and homes, foremost among them Richard Norton, their relative at Rylstone in Wharfedale.

But castles – and houses – can also be regained, as this one was when the Fletcher Norton family bought it back in the mid-eighteenth century, and today, a peaceful farmhouse, it only dreams of the stirring if perilous past evoked by its great hall, its chapel and dungeon.

The same web of political and religious intrigue must have enclosed Markenfield Hall and Fountains Abbey, only a mile or so to the north-west. Heads were no doubt shaken sadly at Markenfield when William Thirsk, the abbot was hanged for his part in the Pilgrimage of Grace. It was William's successor, Marmaduke Bradley, who surrendered the keys of the monastery to Henry VIII on 26 November 1539.

Close your eyes on a summer's night and the echoes of Fountains Abbey return like the ghosts that move silently about these vaulted chambers. But the sound of plainsong that sends a shiver down your spine has no more a ghostly origin than the golden glow of floodlighting with which the Department of the Environment enhances Europe's outstanding monastic ruin for the awesome delight of more than 10,000 visitors every summer.

Even without the artificial effulgence and the recorded music of a monkish mass, the Abbey of St Mary of the Fountains would still be the most popular with tourists of all the Ancient Monuments in the care of the Department in Yorkshire. Once the wealthiest Cistercian house in Britain, it transports us back, as few places can, to the great days of monastic life, when Fountains, like many another monastery, was rich – in this case from its sheep-farming estates and its lead mines in Nidderdale. When Henry VIII graciously accepted its surrender, there went with it 2,356 cattle, 1,326 sheep and 89 pigs – and no doubt splendid horses, too, such as the Cistercians were expert at breeding.

The picture its buildings present of the arrangement of a great religious house is unrivalled. And so much of it is complete – less defaced by time than made venerable in its dignified desuetude.

Fountains was great in every sense, including that of sheer size. Its tower still rises 168 feet, while the church itself is 370 feet long. The east window is 60 feet high; the cloister court, flanked on its east side by four lovely arches, is 125 feet square; the magnificently vaulted cellarium 300 feet long.

The first monks at Fountains sought austerity. They came there to live in a wild and thorny tract of land, beneath the shelter of a single elm, whose leaves they boiled and ate. How they would marvel at its present setting, enhancing the still magnificent water garden begun in 1718 by John Aislabie, whose son William bought the abbey ruins in 1768.

Close by the abbey is the fine Jacobean Fountains Hall, built in 1610 from the ruins of the abbey.

All sorts and conditions of men lie buried at West Tanfield, from the knightly Marmions to one Francis Maximilian Walbran. Not for Francis an alabaster tomb in the ancient church. But perhaps he would not have wanted it. No doubt he's happier beneath the sky in the churchyard, within sound – if he could only hear it – of his beloved Ure, which here marks the boundary between the North and West Ridings of hallowed memory.

The fishing tackle carved in stone at the base of his tombstone gives a clue to how he got there and the lettering fills in the details – 'erected by voluntary subscription . . . accidentally drowned while angling at Tanfield, February 17th, 1909, aged fifty-seven'. At least as moving as, if less noticed than, the armoured effigy inside the church. And how touching that the local folk, who always loved a sportsman, should pay for his tombstone.

The Marmion Tower, a small, battlemented castle gatehouse beside the church, was splinted with scaffolding on the Ure-ward side, providing just the slightest shock, for here the view from the bridge across the Ure is among the most familiar in Yorkshire. And the scaffolding was a recent intrusion.

Undoubtedly the tombs within the church are impressive, but the castle occupied by the family they commemorate vanished long ago. A wrought-iron hearse with prickets for candles (said to be unique in England) encloses Derbyshire alabaster effigies of Sir John Marmion who died in 1387 and his wife, Elizabeth, who followed him and his plate armour and his knightly lion into history a dozen or so years later. How ghostly they would look at midnight with the candles lighted, as sometimes, I believe, they are.

Almost due north of here is Well, a charming hillside village with colourful cottage gardens. Need I say that the village is named from an ancient well, St Michael's. Also ancient, in foundation at least, is the row of almshouses near the church, with at one end a tiny chapel and in the middle, a communal pump. Above the cottages is the date 1758, the fourth figure so eroded as to be almost unreadable.

Adjoining the church is all that remains of Ralph Neville's original Hospital of St Michael the Archangel, where lived the 'cremets', who, though labouring under a name reminiscent of science-fiction, were simply 12 poor men and 12 poor women who lived there under a master and served by two priests, whose further duty it was to pray for the soul of Ralph and his successors.

The charity said to have been founded six hundred years ago suggests that the Nevilles were merciful as well as mighty – that is, until they lost their lands after the Rising of the North, in 1569, when Nevilles and Percys joined forces in a forlorn attempt to dethrone Elizabeth and restore the old religion.

Nevilles and Percys had stood side by side two centuries before, to rout the Scots at the battle of Neville's Cross and take David, their king, prisoner. That earlier Neville, Ralph – who with Henry Lord Percy, led the English forces – rebuilt Well Church as it stands today.

The window in the South Chapel bearing his arms and those of Percy and Ros was probably given in pious thanks for that victory at Red Hill, close to the Neville fastness at Brancepeth; a victory that may have surprised the victors almost as much as it did the vanquished, for it was not long after Crecy, and England's most formidable bowmen were still in France.

Ralph Neville may well have seen his invasion of David's realm as almost a crusade. Scottish raiders had destroyed churches at West Tanfield, Wath, Kirklington and perhaps at Well, but with the Scots king a prisoner, the raids would surely cease and there seemed good reason for thanksgiving.

But the troubles which exercise men's passions in Well today have nothing to do with religion – or so it would seem from the posters reading NO NEW QUARRY and SAVE OUR VILLAGE. All unaware of the rights and wrongs of the dispute I studied a map stuck on an ancient tree trunk to show me and other visitors and residents the respective positions of the 'New Quarry' and a 'Proposed Quarry'.

Catherine Parr, who became the sixth wife of Henry VIII, doubtless knew the church at Well. She lived from time to time at Snape Castle in the village of Snape, a mile or so almost due north of Well. The castle is apparently divided into flats now, a fact which kindled my envious thoughts. Almost a miniature, at first glance it looks nearly complete, but the older parts are in ruins. You reach them by way of the farmyard beside the castle, a route followed by the faithful Anglicans of Snape to reach the castle chapel which also happens to be their parish church.

Were I lucky enough to live in Snape I should go to church every Sunday – mounting the carpeted stairs and rejoicing when 't'Back End' came round, in the unmistakable fragrance of a country harvest festival.

Or if the sermon proved tedious, revelling in the rich wood carving adorning the walls; or dreaming over the medieval window glass. Or staring up in a most spiritual way at the faint traces which are all that remain of paintings reputedly by Verrio.

A pleasant village, Snape, which doubtless deserves the trophy in the form of a white rose presented to it by the Rural Community Council for being a 'best kept village' in one year or another.

North again to Bedale where the local teenagers were riding motor bikes around the Georgian Bedale Hall, now used as a social and administrative centre. Not that little market towns like this ever needed a 'centre' to sustain their social life. Doubtless the harvest dances that were advertised in shop windows ('Mrs Preston's Band') have been held here for generations and, let us hope, will continue to be. Bedale has held a market for more than seven centuries and the stone cross at the centre of its huge market place has stood there for most of that time.

And from the tower of St Gregory's Church, sentries once watched for the raiding Scots, wishful, perhaps, that St George, who fights his dragon in a fresco in the north aisle, would lend them a hand with more immediate problems.

The rooks' parliament was in noisy session a couple of miles up-dale at Crakehall, noted for its great square green and the splendid patriarchal trees that surrounded it. Some of them – a group of beech, sycamore and elm – stood in the grounds of a house, and had been home since time immemorial to the rooks. Every year the certain sign that spring was on the way had been the sight of rooks mending their nests in readiness for another season of family life.

Then, one February, a local naturalist was amazed to see that instead of repairing their nests they were dismantling them with all haste and taking the twigs across the green to a different group of trees. Could it be Dutch elm disease? Hardly. There were only a few elms in the deserted group and they were healthy enough.

A fortnight later, timber merchants arrived in Crakehall with news that the old rookery trees were to be felled. The house in whose grounds they stood belonged to a trust in the south of England and this was the first anyone in the village had heard of the scheme – apart from the rooks, that is!

Southward lay Masham, where brown leaves were scampering across the enormous market square with its worn stone cross; the bell from the steepled church struck 12 at a pace so leisured that, combined with the smell from Theakston's brewery, it might well have sent me to sleep had I been rash enough to sit down. Theakston's is the birthplace of Old Peculier, a brew whose alleged aphrodisiac qualities were the subject of only the least of the claims made for it by a dedicated consumer!

The old market place is in use again today and the charter which authorises its existence dates back for more than 700 years. Before the fine, largely Norman church was begun, probably in the eleventh century, and added to in the fifteenth, a church was built here in the seventh, when the remarkable Edwin ruled Northumbria.

A link with those days stands in the churchyard in the shape of a seven-foot pillar, once part of a Saxon cross on which you might dimly discern weathered carvings of Christ and his apostles and, in a lower series, the Adoration of the Magi. Or possibly saints. I doubt if we can ever be certain now.

The subjects were perhaps a little easier to determine in 1609 when the wife of Sir Marmaduke Wyvill died and he commemorated her with the erection of the fine monument in the north aisle which depicts them both comfortably reclining while their six sons and two daughters kneel piously at prayer below. Since Sir Marmaduke had still eight years to serve before he joined his wife, his eyes, unlike hers, are open.

Should his calm gaze disconcert you, you may turn your own eyes upwards to the painting above the chancel arch, a Nativity scene – or part of one – reputedly by Sir Joshua Reynolds, which was brought here in 1816 after suffering damage in a fire at Belvoir Castle. At the back of the church a memorial reminds you of the fame of Thomas Mallaby, the Masham bell-founder whose more sonorous memorials reside in bell towers all over Yorkshire.

West lies Colsterdale, surely one of the loveliest of the 'little dales' which grace the Ure valley. Here are villages – Fearby with its green, where the only sound, if there are no children playing there, is the munching of cattle. At Healey, cottages demurely line the roadside; and by way of contrast there is Swinton Castle, set in magnificent parkland through which runs the short river Burn which forms two reservoirs on its 12-mile journey from the slopes of Great Haw to its union with the Ure, south of Masham.

Hardly the place, you might think, to have much affinity with the belching mill chimneys and clattering looms of the Victorian West Riding. But in the days when such chimneys belched and such looms clattered – Lord Masham, a nineteenth-century woolman, acquired castle and grounds and set himself to complete the work of the Danbys, former owners, by enlarging the park laid out in the 1820s by William Danby. Perhaps even more remarkable than William's lakes, streams and woodlands is the Druids' Temple he built to provide work during a time of unemployment.

Frequently the unsuspecting have been taken in by William's temple (near Ilton, on land leased by the Forestry Commission from the Swinton estate), but there was never any intention to deceive. 'Plan of Druids' Temple replica', states a notice unequivocally, 'built about 1820'. And a drawing, based on an original plan by one P.T. Runton, Esq., 1873–1947, explains the whole thing, from the sacrificial altar, via the Phallus, to the Solar Temple and the Tomb.

'Regency Folly', says my map, somewhat dismissively. It may be no Stonehenge, but those scores of great stones and hundreds of smaller ones so laboriously sited must have provided a never-to-be forgotten task for some workless labourers 150 years ago. Were they fascinated by their task or was it just a welcome job, to be spun out as long as it would last? No doubt their reactions varied as much as those of visitors today. Most will find the 'temple' well worth seeing, especially since it is to be found in a pleasant picnic area close to a 'viewpoint' from which you may overlook Leighton Reservoir as it bisects Masham Moor.

In its lower reaches, Colsterdale is as fat and smiling as Eden before the Fall – all farms, gardens and well-tended woodland, but its upper parts are as wild as those are tame, until, at High House, the last farm in the dale, sheltered by pine and silver birch, you might well expect to meet a Druid!

From Masham the A6108 winds north-westward to Leyburn, passing High and Low Ellington and Ellingstring until, curving right and then left, it encloses sparse but gracious ruins in its curve – the remains of what an agent of Henry VIII called 'one of the fairest churches that I have seen'. The church was Jervaulx Abbey, the agent, Arthur Darcy and in his letter to Thomas Cromwell he also praised the horses bred at Jervaulx as 'the tried breed in the North'.

William Lorenzo Christie, once the local squire, on whose land the abbey stood, knew all about those horses and the monks who bred them. He told me their story as we explored his abbey one day just before his hundredth birthday. As he tapped his way among the ancient stones he talked admiringly of the skill of the monks in making Wensleydale cheese from ewes' milk, according to a recipe now lost. The squire of Jervaulx was to live another three years before joining the monks about whom he knew so much, and of whom he wrote in a booklet which visitors to the abbey may still read.

Once this peaceful place was the scene of violent destruction. A mob tried to tear the building down after Adam Sedburgh, the last Abbot, died on Tyburn Hill for his part in the Pilgrimage of Grace. They, and other despoilers who followed, have left little more than the ground plan of this monastery established by monks who came here from Fors near Askrigg. But five of the six marble pillars that supported the chapter house remain to form a little masterpiece of accidental artistry, and on each side of the steps leading to the vanished cloister are the arches that enclosed two windows. There is little else here, except peace.

William Lorenzo Christie is affectionately remembered at a village between Witton Fell and the Ure, called East Witton. Set around a long green, it is a quiet spot today but it has known busier times for it was a fourteenth-century market town.

East Witton leads to Coverham, passing Braithwaite Hall (now owned by the National Trust), a farmhouse dating from the seventeenth century with earthworks of uncertain date on its near 800 acres of farmland and moorland. At Coverham are the fragments of a Pre-monstratensian abbey, built in 1212 to be home to an abbot and 16 monks and now forming part of a private house – with sometimes surprising effect. A good way to use old ruins? Yes, why not?

Here we are in the subsidiary dale of the River Cover, which rises near Great and Little Whernside on the North Moor above Starbotton in Wharfedale. And here in Coverdale was born Miles Coverdale, 1488–1568, one of the medieval scholars who once added lustre to Yorkshire – doubtless a result of the presence here of so many monasteries. He was one of those translators of Scripture (his version was known as the Great Bible) who followed in the steps of Wyclif, called by Foxe, 'the Morning Star of the Reformation' and by some 'the first Protestant'. Wyclif, like Coverdale was a Yorkshireman, though his equally eponymous birthplace, Wycliffe, in Teesdale, is now inside Durham's extended boundary.

From Coverham, parallel routes run on each side of the river. The southernmost road goes by way of Caldbergh and East and West Scrafton (the last being reputedly the birthplace of Lord Darnley, who married Mary Queen of Scots), before crossing a bridge over the Cover to rejoin the old road – once a packhorse track – which crosses the moors to Kettlewell in Wharfedale.

Carlton, near where the two roads converge, is the metropolis of the dale. Henry Constantine, the Coverdale Bard, lived here and on his house a stone tablet dated 14 February 1861 commemorates him with some pious lines.

It was in a Coverdale church – perhaps at Horsehouse – that the almost inevitable voluntary cleaner was at work when I called, heating water for her labours on a paraffin stove. She'd been cleaning that church, she said, for forty years. There were certainly fewer worshippers than when she started, so the services were held once a fortnight now.

'I knew you were northerners', she said approvingly. 'Are you going over Park Rash? . . . It's a bit – notorious.' We were, but first we ate a picnic lunch from a roadside vantage point which overlooked the Cover with its backcloth of deeply convoluted fells.

Not a car or a human soul came our way, for Coverdale is still to some extent a hidden, self-contained world, as it has been for two centuries. Hard to believe, indeed, as we struggled to stay awake though the autumn sunshine came warmly through the car windows, that it was once a busy highway. Soldiers marched here on their way to fight the Scots; nobles and even kings, no doubt, made their panoplied way to Middleham, when its castle was the home of that Neville, Earl of Warwick, who became known as the Kingmaker.

Park Rash, though its gradient is one-in-five, holds few terrors today for the reasonably cautious driver – except of course in the wintry conditions that make any road a hazard; but in the old, horse-powered days there must have been much sweating and many a small calamity.

So, passing Great and Little Whernside, down we went without incident to fetch up at Kettlewell, in Wharfedale.

At Middleham, once known as the Windsor of the North, we meet the Nevilles again – that family who came to England with William the Conqueror and, once here, proceeded to shape the history of England to their own design.

They were big in every sense: and it seems prophetic that having gained Middleham Castle by marriage in the thirteenth century, they soon enlarged on the proportions of the original builder. And no Neville was bigger, either in stature or power, than Richard, Earl of Warwick. The 'Kingmaker' was a king's gaoler, too, for during the Wars of the Roses one king, Edward IV was a prisoner at Middleham.

It is hard now to appreciate the power and pomp of the Nevilles. They were like kings in the palace they created around Ralph Fitzranulph's great Norman keep, 100 feet by 80 feet and with walls 12 feet thick. And what they built astonishes us still; today a ruin, yes, but even as a ruin one of the most famous of English castles. Those curtain walls were once 250 feet long with a tower at each corner.

And one of those towers – the Prince's or Round Tower (as it is named in a sixteenth-century survey) heard in 1473 the first infant cries of Prince Edward, son of Richard, Duke of Gloucester (the future Richard III) who was given Middleham after Warwick's death at the Battle of Barnet in 1471. His last cries, too, for the boy prince died there ten years later and may rest now in Sheriff Hutton's Church of St Helen and Holy Cross, near York. Here a monument is worn from the scraping of ill-sighted and credulous folk who for some reason believed its powdered alabaster would heal their eyes.

There are those, though, who say the young prince lies at Middleham and that his monument, made at York, reached Sheriff Hutton only after King Richard's death in 1485 at Bosworth Field and was raised there because its transporters dared not go further on the road to Middleham for fear of Henry Tudor, final victor in the Wars of the Roses which had lasted for thirty years and spilt much blood on Yorkshire soil.

What sort of man *was* Richard? Was he deformed? Did he merit Shakespeare's description:

> *Cheated of feature by dissembling nature,*
> *Deform'd, unfinish'd, sent before my time*
> *Into this breathing world scarce half made up,*

or was it simply that over-zealous practice at jousting and martial training with battle-axe, sword and dagger had caused excessive development of his right shoulder and arm? He was comely enough, said some who knew him in his youth but of 'low stature', and there was the Scottish envoy, who declared that never had nature enclosed a greater mind in so small a frame. But then, it was advisable to flatter princes.

Without doubt a better testimonial was the love felt for Richard by the common folk of Middleham who cheered when Warwick's daughter, Anne Neville, Richard's cousin and childhood companion became his devoted wife on the death of her husband, Richard's brother, the Prince of Wales – a death of which Richard himself was to be accused, just as he was accused of the deaths of his nephews, the two Princes in the Tower. Middleham folk would have none of that. Nor would the Fellowship of the White Boar, which still works to restore Richard's good name (a white boar being the heraldic emblem of Richard which still adorns the Boar Cross, one of Middleham's two market crosses).

Or is it a boar? A plaque tells you that the Boar Cross is believed to commemorate the grant obtained by Richard for Middleham in 1479 of a fair and market twice yearly, and that the sculptured animal, now sadly eroded, may be his own cognisance of the White Boar 'or the emblem of the family of his wife Anne Neville, co-heiress of the lordship of Middleham'. Small wonder that, with such distinguished patronage, Middleham was in its day the capital of Wensleydale.

When, at the Battle of Bosworth in 1485, Richard 'was piteously slain and murdered to the great heaviness of this City' (as York's aldermen lamented) the castle became Crown property and remained so until 1604, when it was given to Henry Lindley by King James I. In 1569 came the Rising of the North. It failed and the reign of the Nevilles died with it.

During the Civil War Middleham Castle became just another of the ruins that Cromwell 'knocked abaht a bit!' He made a particular point of knocking them about in the north, so that they were less likely to cause him trouble. But in Middleham's case, though the castle was now almost a ruin through neglect, the great walls stood firm against the Round-heads' powder. And many a ghostly Neville may have smiled. . . .

Richard's present-day supporters have left a colourful mark in Middleham Church where a stained glass window in the south aisle, near the door, pleads mutely for Richard's good reputation. How surprised he might be by it all if he should visit the church and be pointed out to himself as the figure kneeling at the foot of the window with his son Edward and Anne Neville, his wife. The window dates from 1934 and almost 30 years later the Fellowship of the White Boar added a green altar frontal, again in honour of the king they believe has been so maligned.

Perhaps Richard would consider his window a fitting adornment for the church. After all, it was he who raised its status to that of a collegiate church with a dean and six canons, the last of whom, Charles Kingsley, has closer links with Malhamdale than with Wensleydale, for it was there that he found inspiration to write *The Water Babies*.

Not far from the church you will see Kingsley House and also St Alkelda's Cottage and will remember that the church is dedicated to St Mary and St Alkelda, a beautiful Anglian princess, martyred for her faith by heathen Viking women who strangled her with her own long golden hair. Her grave lies beneath the floor of the church.

A few miles to the north west, Leyburn, surely the present capital of Wensleydale, stands at a crossroads where four roads meet, one of them the road we have travelled from Ripon and the great bustling centres of Leeds and Bradford. Then there is the road eastward to Northallerton and ultimately Middlesbrough and the coast; as well as the highway to Richmond and the north, while westward winds the main road through Wensleydale and on to Garsdale and eventually the Lakes. Meanwhile we explore Leyburn.

It has had a market since Charles II presented it with a market charter (presumably at the request of the man who became Duke of Bolton) and never, surely, was the big market place busier than it is today on Fridays. Today you won't see the cross, the stocks and the bull ring that once stood here. That might suggest that the market folk of Leyburn have no time for such sentimental relics of the past. Be that as it may, the town centre is now a Conservation Area, no doubt to the great satisfaction of the Council for British Archaeology, who in 1965 declared that the ancient heart of Leyburn should be treated with the care and respect due to venerable old age.

And if the stocks and the bull ring are gone, the vast market place retains the cobbles where livestock used to be sold; though since 1917 that function has been filled by the auction mart to the north of the town.

I never think of Leyburn without recalling Leyburn Shawl and therefore Fred Lawson, who, not far from here, at Castle Bolton, showed me his painting called 'The Road to Leyburn Shawl'. Fred was a king among Dales artists and we shall enter his former village kingdom in due time. Meanwhile, what was, or is, Leyburn Shawl?

It is a long natural terrace behind the town, running parallel with the valley and affording the most superb views of Wensleydale. But more romantic associations are hinted at in the name of a spot called 'Queen's Gap'.

In 1568, after her defeat at Langside, the tragic Mary Queen of Scots was brought to Bolton's grim, four-square moatless fortress, and here she stayed for half a year – but as no willing guest. . . . It was a Dalesman, Kit Norton, of Rylstone, son of one of the most staunchly Catholic families of the Dales, who connived at her escape. Having given her guards the slip one night, Mary's hopes were high – but only for two hours. They captured her at Queen's Gap on this daleside terrace, which gained its name, some say, because here Mary lost her hope of freedom – and her shawl.

A pity that, like most good stories, this one is squashed as flat as the poor Queen's hopes! The word 'shawl', we are told is derived from *schalls*, a version of *skali*, which is a Scandinavian word for the huts or shelters once used here by Norse settlers; for this area has given shelter to human beings since prehistoric times. Below the Shawl are the foundations – shaped like horseshoes – of early hunters' houses. Here, too, are Ancient British earthworks and the simple tools of long dead men. So . . . you relinquish a romantic tale and find a truth perhaps more exciting.

A mile or so south-east of Leyburn is Spennithorne, whose church-yard boasts, of all things a Russian cross from Sebastopol. It surmounts the vault of the Van Straubenzee family, one of whose number, General Sir Charles Van Straubenzee, commanded a British brigade during the Crimean War. Inside the church a picture recalling the sacking of Sebastopol by the British shows the golden cross falling from the chapel during the fighting.

Wensley, a mile or two north-west is one of the sweetest villages in the dale that bears its name. Once *this* was the busy market town of Wensleydale, and Leyburn a mere village. But the church register records the visitation in 1563 of a plague, 'most hote and fearful so that many fled and the Town of Wensley by reason of the sickness was unfrequented for a long season'. Some of the villagers moved to Leyburn whither Wensley's market (already more than two centuries old) followed them; but all too many travelled no farther than Chapel Hill (or Field), where they were taken to be buried.

Many prayers must have been said in Wensley's Church of the Holy and Undivided Trinity in those sad days. It has been called the finest church in the Dales – a large claim, but not a surprising one. There was a church here when Wensley was the Wendeslaga of the Anglo-Saxons – an Anglo-Danish structure which was replaced, at least as early as the thirteenth century, by the building of which so much survives today. It is hard to say what is the greatest glory of this lovely church – the carving of the old pews and chancel stalls by the same hands that fashioned Ripon Cathedral's misericord seats; the reliquary which may once have held the remains of Agatha, Easby Abbey's patron saint; the exquisitely carved parclose screen from that same abbey, or what are said to be the earliest church murals in Yorkshire.

Wensley was once a centre of religious art, where carvers pursued their intricate craft under the inspiration of Italian artists brought to England at the behest of that most dynamic of early churchmen and Yoredale saints, Wilfrid of Ripon.

Later than these are the Bolton family pews, contained in a kind of raised box, screened and curtained, whose design was possibly based by a lovesick Duke of Bolton on the theatre box from which he listened, enchanted, to the delectable cadences of Lavinia Fenton, first Polly Peachum in John Gay's *Beggar's Opera*.

That, at least, was the account given to me by a man I met one day in Wensley and it seems too good a story to doubt. In any case, Lavinia became in due time the Duchess of Bolton, and from Polly Peachum's Tower, still to be seen two miles from Bolton Hall, she sang for her husband and his guests as they sat in the grounds of the hall.

Wensley seems to have grouped itself about Bolton Hall, which stands in its wooded park between Wensley and its neighbour village, Redmire. The family built it in 1678, as their old home, Bolton Castle, was no longer habitable after its 'slighting' in the Civil War. (When the north-east tower of the castle suddenly collapsed in 1761 they must have congratulated themselves on having made a wise move.)

Three miles west of Wensley, Redmire is most pleasantly reached by way of the tree-shaded park of Bolton Hall, beside which the Ure takes its leisured course.

Redmire. . . . If ever a village deserved a better name this one does. A changeless, seemingly sleepy spot where the only sound on my last visit came from an aged sheepdog barking incessantly from a farm gate bordering the green – complaining perhaps because nowadays that was all he *could* do. Did I say changeless? Not quite: a pillar on the green bears a notice informing you that its erection marked the occasion when the village was supplied with lamps to mark Queen Victoria's Golden Jubilee; while another notice on the same pillar records that the pillar itself was fitted with an electric light to commemorate the Silver Jubilee of Elizabeth II. And lamps may still be seen bracketed to some houses to light up the streets which radiate from the little village green.

So something *does* happen sometimes at Redmire, even if it takes a royal jubilee to bring it about. Thus the casual townee visitor might conclude – and what a superficial judgement that would be. For plenty happens here, even if the old Redmire Feast with its races and wrestling and face-pulling contests is no more. The country, need I say it, is where 'the action' takes place and if the conviviality of the Bolton Arms or the King's Arms is not to your taste, there is more demanding activity for those who want it: 'Lecture tonight at St Oswald's Exhibition Centre, Castle Bolton: Lead-mining in early prints' reads a notice at the little village hall. And we may be sure the lecturer, Dr Arthur Raistrick, did not lack an appreciative audience.

Such an authority could easily have answered questions about another aspect of the district's past, the discovery at Redmire of a sulphur well, which gave rise in some quarters to the ambition to make Redmire a spa to rival Harrogate. However (as also happened in the much less spa-like setting of Ossett in the West Riding), such dreams were soon forgotten – perhaps because Redmire was too busy being itself to try to realise them. And for *that* I'm thankful.

A mile or so to the west, Castle Bolton recalls for me Fred Lawson (remember his painting of Leyburn Shawl?) and Muriel Metcalfe, his wife, also a painter, whom I visited many years ago at their low-ceilinged cottage.

Fred, a John Bull of a man with cheeks weathered to the colour of ripe cherries, went to Castle Bolton in 1910 'for a month' and stayed all his life. At one time he worked in oils, but painting in the Dales with their rapid changes of weather and sky calls for mobility. So he stopped using oils – 'it was too heavy, carrying all that paraphernalia about with me' – and began to work chiefly in water-colour and pen and ink.

Conversation in the Lawsons' cottage (as I found twenty years ago) was an enriching experience, the more so, no doubt, when their daughter Sonia was with them, for she too is an artist who has grown steadily in reputation during the intervening years, and she too paints the Dales and Bolton Castle, though naturally in a different style from her parents.

Long before it became the home of the Boltons, the castle, whose massive bulk is unmistakably visible from many points, was home to the Scropes, one of the most powerful families in medieval England. Probably of Norman extraction, they were at Wensley by 1205 and by 1285 owned land at Castle Bolton (East Bolton as it was called then).

Sir Geoffrey le Scrope, one of the family's distinguished lawyers, was an adviser to Edward II and Edward III. But he was a man of action, too, distinguished as a soldier and as a knight of tournaments. And he was a diplomat, undertaking missions to the Netherlands, France and Scotland, one of which, in 1328, culminated in the recognition of Scotland's independence.

Sir Geoffrey's nephew, Richard, built Bolton Castle; his grandson, also Richard, became Archbishop of York, one of the three prelates in a family which produced, among a host of luminaries, two earls, twenty barons, two Chief Justices, a Chancellor and five Knights of the Garter.

Nearly two hundred years before the first Lord Scrope was given a licence in 1379 to crenellate his house at Bolton, a preceptory of the Knights Templar was established at Swinithwaite, a few miles to the south-east.

When the order was dissolved in 1312 the preceptory was handed over to the Hospitallers. They, too, came and went, leaving their chapel to fall in ruins about the graves of the knights who once worshipped there; and to be forgotten until 1840, when the remains were discovered.

Swinithwaite, at the foot of Penhill, which rises to nearly 1,800 feet has that name for one of two reasons. It means, say some authorities, confidently, 'a forest clearing for the feeding or impounding of wild swine', others take the view, less obvious, perhaps, that the *Swini* part of the name is possibly a personal name of Norse-Irish origin. But there is no doubt that *thwaite* signifies a woodland clearing or a field sloping to a valley bottom.

Swinithwaite has clearly been here a long, long time. There is little to see at the village itself, though Temple Farm (the reason for whose name can be in *no* doubt) dates back to 1608 and may once have served Wensleydale travellers as a coaching inn.

West Witton, a mile or two east of here, is where they burn Owd Bartle, though just who he was I don't pretend to know. The wiseacres will tell you that the unseasonal Guy Fawkes who meets a fiery end here every year represents St Bartholomew, the patron saint of the parish church. True, the bonfire brightens the late August sky on the Saturday after St Bartholomew's Day, but why should anyone wish to cremate the effigy of this good man who almost certainly never did West Witton any harm?

At ten o'clock on the appointed night, Owd Bartle begins his annual journey to destruction at the head of a procession along the length of the village. And as his devotees carry him, they chant his disastrous history –

> *At Pen Hill Crags he tore his rags,*
> *At Hunter's Thorn he blew his horn,*
> *At Capplebank Stee he brake his knee,*
> *At Grisgill Beck he brake his neck,*

At Wadham's End he couldn't fend,
At Grisgill End he made his end.

And at Grisgill (or Grass Gill) End he does precisely that in a dying glory of smoke and flame.

Travel up-dale a few miles to the west and a road to the left will lead you to the 'little dale' of Bishopdale, through which travellers from Wharfedale to Wensleydale pass along the B6160. The road from Buckden climbs to the summit of Kidstones Pass (1,400 feet) then drops to accompany the Bishopdale Beck past limestone scars and farms whose datestones proclaim them to be two and sometimes three centuries old – like West New House, which, despite its name, is the oldest house in Bishopdale. This wonderfully preserved example of a Pennine 'long house' was built in 1635. Not far from here, at Foss Gill, a series of 14 waterfalls hands the beck down 800 feet from High Scar.

Near the Street Head Inn a road leads off to the village of Newbiggin. A relic of coaching times, the inn is one of the oldest in the Dales, proud that its original oak beams are still as good, it seems, as they were in 1730 when the hostelry was established. Once this road was the only one to the village, but now another road from Newbiggin takes you back to the B6160, which you may cross to reach Thoralby, with its listed village hall, which dates from 1704.

A mile or so due north of Thoralby is Aysgarth, renowned for its falls – Upper, Middle and Lower. They are best seen, I suggest, on a bright autumn day when the blue of the sky, the gold of the leaves and the silver of the sun reflects in the water – white as it roars over broad limestone steps, brown as it emerges from beneath the bridge, some centuries old, that offers the best vantage point from which to view the Upper Falls.

Close to the meeting of Bishopdale with her smaller sister, Waldendale, West Burton, at the foot of the 1,792-foot Penhill, is one of the loveliest villages in Wensleydale – with one of the largest village greens, I would think, in all Yorkshire. Here the children of the village school play team games on a 'playground' of rare charm.

As the tapering cross on the green suggests, there was a time when this quietest of Dales villages was busy once a week with market traders. But those days are now long past, and the present cross, built in 1820 and restored in 1889, could be said to be relatively brand new.

You cross a bridge over the Walden Beck to follow a path to the spot nearby, where the beck cascades into a limestone-walled, tree-shaded basin.

Wild Waldendale this used to be – the last refuge in Yorkshire of the wild red deer and the pine martin – and it remains a lonely, hidden place, at least to the multitude.

Just south of West Burton the road divides into two to flank the

Walden beck as it takes its course to its union with the Bishopdale Beck and finally with the Ure. It first gathers itself into a stream on Buckden Pike, to fall and splash two miles over Walden Moor to Walden Head, a thousand feet lower and – Kentucky!

There are few buildings at Walden Head; Kentucky House – however it got its name – is one of them: a farm, of course. The road inclines north-east, with every mile or so a farm, traversing a scattered graveyard of forgotten miles until it merges, less than a mile from West Burton, with its shorter companion road that flanks the beck on its eastern side.

This, too, travels in the society of abandoned mine-workings and boasts as a landmark the chimney of West Burton Mill where lead was smelted. From Cote Farm a track leads to Carlton and, by way of Horsehouse, to Starbotton and Kettlewell in Wharfedale.

Westward (on the northern side of the main dale) lies Carperby with its Friends Meeting House, built in 1864. Its silence is broken now only by the ticking of a clock that stands in one corner of the room opposite a figure of Elizabeth Fry, benign yet strong-featured in her Quaker grey.

'Straggling' seems too harsh a word to apply to Carperby, and indeed, its successes in 'Best Kept Village' contests (in 1959 it was the first Dales village so honoured) suggests that it is a comely place, as indeed it is. When the rough, seventeenth-century cross, reached by steps on the green, was erected, Carperby's market was already old, with a charter granted in 1303. And still to be seen on the hillsides above the village are the lynchets or terraces, now overgrown, left in many areas of the Dales both by Danish and Anglian ploughmen as they toiled to make a team of perhaps eight oxen follow a straight course over the sloping land.

The Dales are not over-rich in prehistoric remains, yet near here – on Oxclose Pasture, under Nab End – is the largest stone circle in the Dales, a mysterious relic of the Early Bronze Age 'Dalesmen' who came here in about 1800 BC from the Continent by way of Ireland. Most of the original 16 or so stones are still *in situ* (unusual in itself when such stones provided useful building material) and though some of those stones are fallen, the 'circle' remains – if not quite a perfect circle, for it measures 92 feet long by 78 feet wide.

The road between Carperby and Askrigg passes Nappa Hall, a fortified manor built in the fifteenth century, which became, in Leland's phrase 'the chilliest house of the Metcalfes'. Its builder was Thomas of that populous clan, who can fairly be said to have made his family a power in the land – certainly in Wensleydale.

Nappa Hall is not open to the public. When I last saw it, it was leading a workaday existence as a farmhouse, little changed in appearance since

James built it: basically it is a single-storey banqueting hall flanked by two battlemented towers, the taller, western one being the older, for the south wing was added in the seventeenth century.

Mary Queen of Scots knew Nappa for a time. So, less briefly, did the redoubtable Anne Clifford, whom we met in Airedale, and who must have cast a discerning eye over the place, for castles meant much in Lady Anne's life. She was born, you recall, at Skipton Castle in 1590. Thirty-three years later, while travelling from there to her castle at Brougham in Westmorland, she went from Barden Tower in Wharfedale, to Nappa. And she confided to her diary that it was the first time she had ever been in 'Kettlewell dale' or had travelled over Stake Pass, and thanked God for preserving her on such a perilous journey. I wonder how comfortably she travelled, for sometimes she rode in a coach, sometimes in a horse litter, but always with a cavalcade of almost royal splendour – one coach for maidservants, another for ladies-in-waiting, while menservants rode on horseback. Thomas Metcalfe, her cousin, possibly looked forward to her visits – or possibly not! At least her arrivals and departures would hardly go unnoticed. . . .

Almost two centuries before Lady Anne was born, James Metcalfe left his native Wensleydale village, Worton, to fight the French with his lord, Sir Richard Scrope of Bolton Castle. But James had more on his mind than fighting. He was appointed Sir Richard's quartermaster and built up a flourishing trade in booty on the side. He became so rich that when Sir Richard was short of money he borrowed from James and so arrived home heavily in his debt. In lieu of money, he repaid the debt by giving James the Nappa estate, whereupon James's son Thomas built Nappa Hall. Soon Thomas added more land to his possessions, and since there was never in Wensleydale a shortage of 'Meccas' (as Metcalfes were known) he installed them in farms and houses on the lands he now could call his own.

With prosperity came honour for the Metcalfes. James himself became Wensleydale's Chief Forester. The tribe had progressed so far in 1555 that in that year Sir Christopher Metcalfe became High Sheriff of York. He rode into that city to accept the office, followed by more than 300 men – every one of them a Metcalfe, and each riding a white horse.

The Metcalfes were a rumbustious clan, least likely to be in trouble when they could involve themselves in warfare, at home or abroad. At Flodden they gained bloody glory against the Scots; in England they supported the Yorkists during the Wars of the Roses. Doubtless they would have been fined for it, too, like many other Yorkshire family when the Lancastrians claimed final victory through the accession of Henry VII – except that, being Metcalfes, they were too clever. When a Metcalfe was threatened with sequestration of his lands he would promptly sell his possessions for a shilling – to another Metcalfe, of course – and buy them back when the trouble had blown over. Even when the hangman's noose threatened, Metcalfe money more than once proved efficacious.

The Metcalfes reigned in Wensleydale like kings – for a time. Some say that it was the somewhat ostentatious Christopher, who made such a show with 300 white horses when he became High Sheriff of York, who began the dissipation of the family's wealth. But if the Metcalfes never quite recovered the glory which began with James and Nappa Hall, there are still plenty of them around.

Had you been a lovelorn youth living in Askrigg long years ago you might not have sent your sweetheart a posy of flowers, or even a valentine. More probably you would have presented her with a knitting sheath, painstakingly and lovingly carved in leisure moments. For Askrigg, like many another Dales village, was famed for its knitters and its knitting. Not as famous as Dent Town in Dentdale but as Askrigg might have told you, they were not so 'knittin' mad' as the folk in Dent!

Askrigg went in also for brewing, cotton spinning, dyeing and – less well known perhaps – clock-making. Even so, they still found time for knitting, using not only two needles but the knitting sheath, too, in the form of a hollow, carved piece of wood fixed in a belt called a cowband and used to support a third needle. Many a knitting sheath is now a family heirloom, whilst others are to be seen in Yorkshire museums.

In those early days Askrigg was very much a self-contained community, and it is taking steps to become one again – to some extent at least. And this largely thanks to the present vicar, Malcolm Stonestreet. With his help has been launched the Askrigg Foundation, which recently turned a derelict mill into a residential youth centre and opened a craft shop selling locally produced goods. Knitting products still have their place, but the sweaters now have to compete with lampshades, marmalade and watercolours.

There is no market now in Askrigg: it died when Hawes assumed prominence as a result of the construction of the turnpike. But the market cross with its many steps still stands outside the churchyard, and close by is the iron ring where bulls were tethered to be baited for the amusement of spectators, some of whom watched from a safe and privileged vantage point – the balustraded balcony of William Thornton's lovely Jacobean house. He built it in 1678, erecting the balcony linking the two wings for the express purpose, so it is said, of providing a grandstand for his 'sporting' guests. Sadly, the mullioned windows of Thornton's house – with its timber beams, gables and nail-studded doors – no longer look out upon Askrigg's market place, for it was destroyed by fire in 1935.

Jack Metcalfe, a few miles away at Bainbridge, is a living link with the 'Meccas' commemorated at Askrigg Church – one of many, of course, but Jack is special, for he personally perpetuates a custom which has possibly been observed in the dale since a relation of William the Conqueror first appointed forest-keepers there.

Their duties included the blowing of a horn to guide travellers through wild country during the dark and dangerous months from Holyrood to Shrovetide. And since you can hardly imagine the Metcalfes of those days letting anybody else in on such a jolly (not to say noisy) activity, it had to be a Metcalfe who blew the horn – and it still has. They say, rightly or otherwise, that no-one but a Metcalfe can hit a top C or make the sound carry a full three miles!

Years ago Jack talked to me about his traditional task and blew the handsome instrument – its note has been compared with both a cow and a banshee – from Bainbridge village green. That particular horn was a hundred years old and Jack was well into his seventies, but the deep note echoed as truly as ever across the fells.

Being little more than a century old, this horn, with its silver bands and chain, is not the first of the Wensleydale forest horns, and one of its predecessors hangs in Castle Bolton Museum. I'm not sure which of the two horns appeared in the photograph shown me by Jack, in which one of his predecessors ostensibly blows the long instrument from a sitting position while nonchalantly leaning one elbow on an imitation pillar in some Victorian photographer's studio. But I would hazard a guess that the 'blast', on that occasion was silent. Even a Metcalfe, I imagine, has to stand up to this job!

Not all Bainbridge institutions have remained as true to tradition as the horn-blowing. It seems almost a sacrilege to me that motor-cycles have taken a large share of the Bainbridge Sports, which nearly 50 years ago just made ends meet on a programme consisting mainly of quoits, clay pigeon shooting and a fell race. Today, the event is almost 'big business', by comparison, drawing folk from hundreds of miles away to see the trotting races and other events.

Almost as much an institution as the horn is the Rose and Crown, where it hangs when off-duty. The inn overlooking the green has been a refuge for Dales travellers for at least five centuries – though that hardly seems so long when you contemplate the site of the Roman fort on Brough Hill, east of the village. Virosidum it was called, and a cohort of 500 soldiers occupied its two-and-a-half acres for roughly three centuries from 80 years after the birth of Christ.

Their marching steps sounded on the direct road they used between here and the Roman settlement called Isurium at Aldborough, near

Boroughbridge. It took them over Wether Fell to Ribblehead, Lancaster and Ribchester – the Cam Road – and part of it, called Gearstones, is followed by present-day Pennine Way walkers who pass Cam Houses, 1,500 feet up Cam Fell, with its claim to be the loneliest, as well as the highest, farm in Yorkshire.

Almost due south of Bainbridge is Addlebrough, a miniature Table Mountain, nearly 1,600 feet high, which was used as a summer camp by the Romans stationed at Brough Hill.

Bainbridge takes its name from the little River Bain, at two miles long the shortest river in England. And from the bridge, that spans it may be seen Bain Fall, where the waters cascade over a great, crescent-shaped slab of Yoredale limestone.

Bain has its birth in Semerwater, a lake as lovely as its name. It floats in a hollow of the hills as serene as the swans, reflected white upon its mirror surface – unless a storm raises its slumbering anger. Where did it come from? Well, a beggar, refused alms at a city which once stood here, called down the wrath of heaven upon its inhabitants. The rains came, and now there is no city – only Semerwater. (A fair exchange, I would say.) That at least is what men believed for centuries, but you may, if gullible, listen to those who say that a glacier formed it in the ice-bound ages.

Whatever its origin, now the streams from Raydale, Bardale and Cragdale feed it. Just why the little River Bain should choose to seek its freedom by boring through the moraine I don't pretend to know; but it soon grows lonely and seeks the company of the Ure.

Ill-naturedly I begrudge Semerwater to the crowds who at weekends and holidays sail motor-boats here and ride water-skis. They sunbathe on the Carlow-Stone, once thrown by a giant at the devil, and propel their noisy craft over the water without a thought about the sunken city which legend locates beneath them. I wish they'd take their noisy playthings somewhere else! And so, surely, do the ghosts of Semerdale (the Quaker Dale, it might be called) whose presence can be felt in the middle of a winter week when you (or I) and the swans have the place to ourselves.

I wish I were a good enough ornithologist to recognise all the 30 or so species of birds noted on Semerwater's shores by John Fothergill, who was born in 1712 at Carr End Farm near it southern end. Benjamin Franklin said that Quaker Fothergill was 'a great doer of good' – but that doesn't tell you the half of it! John left Sedbergh School to become apprentice to a Bradford apothecary. He qualified as a doctor at Edinburgh and began practising in London when he was about 26. Success in the treatment of victims of a sore throat epidemic soon resulted in his practice becoming one of the largest in the capital.

Fothergill's earnings as a physician made him a wealthy man, but as he pointed out to his friends, he would as soon have practised medicine for financial gain as he would have resorted to vice or intemperance. His indifference to personal profit was made manifest when he declined to go to Russia to inoculate the empress against smallpox, recommending, instead, another physician, who acquired both riches and honours by undertaking the task.

Fothergill tried (with other Quakers) to prevent the American War of Independence; worked for prison reform with John Howard, after whom the Howard League is named, and tirelessly demanded that London streets should be made wider to reduce fire hazards.

Perhaps he had time to achieve so much because he remained a bachelor! And we can be thankful that he did, because his sister Ann, who went to London to keep house for him and furnish him with good Yorkshire cooking, was an indefatigable letter-writer and diarist and it is largely through her that we have been left a full and vivid account of his life.

When he was about 50 he began his botanical gardens at Upton, which are said to have rivalled Kew in the rarity and variety of the plants he grew there. A many-sided man indeed. But in Yorkshire he will always be remembered chiefly as the founder of the Quaker School at Ackworth near Pontefract.

John Fothergill was born two years after the Quakers of Semerdale built their meeting house beside the green at tiny Countersett at the northern end of the lake; and doubtless as an infant he was taken with the other children of John and Margaret, his worthy yeoman parents, along the lake-bordering road to Sunday meeting there. The meeting house is still in use, though now, in the true spirit of the Friendly Persuasion, it is available to the Methodists, too.

Close by is Countersett Hall. Here, in the reign of Charles II, lived Richard Robinson, the first Quaker of Wensleydale. As one of the eleven trustees of the Manor of Bainbridge. Richard travelled to London to purchase the royalties from the citizens of London, to whom the hard-up Charles I had conveyed the Manor in 1628.

Two roads from Bainbridge, between which runs the Bain, take you to Semerwater. The road east of the little river traverses a succession of pastures around the feet of Addlebrough before reaching 'Busk' – Stalling Busk to give the village its full title – an ancient settlement. Between this hamlet and the lake – much smaller since 1937 when, strangely, Semerwater was drained for the sake of land reclamation – there rises gauntly a ruin which might be the remains of a farm or a cowshed were it not for the square bell turret which perches – like a cock-eyed chimney stack say some – atop the crumbling walls.

On this site in 1603 was built a church for Semerdale; it was rebuilt in

1722, but many winters and summers have turned the fells white and green since services were held there, and now only these broken walls remain.

And yet, at times, visitors have felt their scalps tingle as they have stood near these walls and heard, unmistakably, the sound of voices singing hymns. Closer inspection of the lakeside reveals nothing ghostly, but a Semerwater scene with Galilean echoes as a local vicar preaches from a boat to a congregation of hundreds fringing the lakeside. It happens once every year on a summer Sunday. On that day the vicar of Askrigg and Stalling Busk has surely his biggest congregation of the year.

The motor-boats are silent then; from the wooden pier children dangle their feet in the water; the water-skiers, willingly or not, stop skating like human insects on the glittering surface, and all join in singing the hymns played by a local band.

'Busk' has a 'new' church now, said by some to be the smallest parish church in England.

From Busk walkers follow a high road or a low, though 'road' is perhaps the wrong word for the track which climbs Cragdale to join Stake Pass, truly a high way to Wharfedale while the downward road fords Bardale Beck to reach Marsett – a chapel, a group of farms and a cow-spotted green.

Marsett, Countersett, Appersett, Burtersett – the suffix *sett* proves the antiquity of settlements such as these, for they are of Norse origin and date back to the early tenth century. On some old maps, *sett* appears as 'side', a *side* being a clearing in the forest which once clothed these fells. A homely usage, this, which will not fall strangely on the Yorkshire ears of those who were told as children to 'side' (or clear away) their toys. Such *setts* or *sides* were used as spring and summer grazing fields, or shielings.

Hereabouts the Bardale Beck ends its journey through its own delectable little dale to join Cragdale Water and the Raydale Beck, which feed Semerwater before they reissue at the far side of the lake as the River Bain.

A few miles west of Bainbridge, Hawes perches among its attendant fells – Lovely Seat, Great Shunner, Dodd Fell: Hawes, the second highest market town in England and the highest in Yorkshire.

Among the most interesting things in Hawes is Kit Calvert's bookshop – after Kit himself, that is. Kit is a busy man, even in retirement and often absent from the shop. And so, on a table in the middle of the floor is a box with a notice thereon reading PLEASE PLACE VALUE OF BOOKS IN THIS BOX. THANK YOU. In the unlikely event of any of my readers being burglariously inclined I should point out that the box is locked and fastened to the table.

That table is flanked by two chairs of apparently oriental design, so you may sit comfortably while you browse, whether your choice be an ancient *Girl Guide Annual,* a life of Florence Nightingale or a brochure printed to commemorate the golden jubilee of the Rotary Club of Glasgow - 1912-62. Unlikely sharers of space on the table and shelves are the *Arabian Nights Dreambook, Senior School Mathematics, Divine Immanence* and a set of ancient encyclopaedias.

As a good Yorkshireman and undeniably a first-rate businessman, Kit takes pleasure in telling you how even the most abstruse tome will often find a buyer if you wait long enough. Nobody will ever persuade me that he keeps his bookshop mainly from commercial motives, and he readily admits, in fact, that he loses money on it. His love of books probably dates from the age of nine, when after much insistence from Kit, his father bought him a dictionary. It cost ten pence, which was no small amount to a quarryman earning at the best 18 shillings a week.

Out of the 18 shillings Kit's Dad paid a shilling a week in rent for their cottage at Burtersett and somehow found a few coppers for Kit's schooling. He would surely feel today that the money had been well invested.

'I still have that dictionary', Kit told me once. I don't doubt it.

How proud Kit's quarryman father would have been to see his son honoured by the award of the M.B.E. for services to the community, an occasion which found Kit resplendent in grey topper and morning suit – rather a change from the battered trilby, boots and old jacket which, with a somewhat abbreviated clay pipe, make up his usual uniform.

Kit Calvert might be said to be Wensleydale personified. What else can you say about a man who not only saved the Wensleydale cheese industry from extinction but whose translation of parts of the New Testament into the Wensleydale dialect found a permanent place in B.B.C. archives? He has recently added the Twenty-third Psalm to his various New Testament translations – 'Evan if Ah cu' t' deeath's deursteead Ahs nut bi freetend, fer He'll bi wi' me. His creuk an' esh plant 'll uphod me. . . .'

Kit never had any illusions about the necessity of work. Money was so short in his boyhood that meat was for Sunday dinner only and even then it had to help out in Dad's sandwiches during the week. So he soon found himself working as a butcher's boy – just for his supper. Years passed and he became a farmer. The year 1935 saw him founding the Wensleydale Cheese Joint Conference in order to replace the spirit of competition among the farmers with an attitude of co-operation. That saved the cheese industry for the time being, but in just a few years it was to face another threat. And this time, but for Kit Calvert, the industry might have died completely.

17 Hardraw Force, the highest single-drop waterfall in England

18 Masham. The steepled church is rich in interest. In the churchyard an ancient
pillar forms a link with the little town's earliest days

19 Ripon Cathedral. Outside, the dour strength of millstone grit; within, the fantasies of ancient woodcarving

20 Middleham Castle, home of the Nevilles and once the prison of a king

21 Fountains Abbey, 'built on wool', was once the richest Cistercian house in Britain

22 Nappa Hall, built by Thomas Metcalfe, one of the rumbustious and proliferous Wensleydale clan

23 Snape Castle, once home to Catherine Parr, last wife of Henry VIII

24 Muker, in Swaledale, where the Keartons went to school

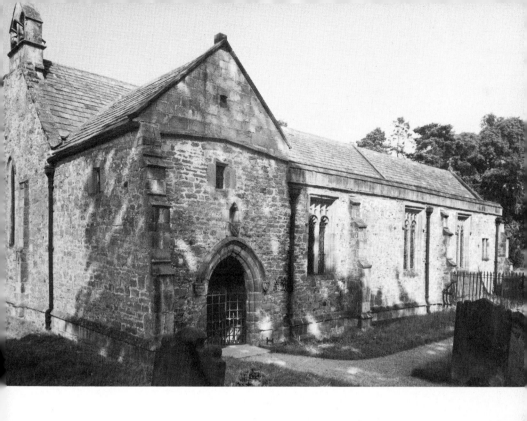

25 Easby Church has frescoes dating from the thirteenth century

26 Easby Abbey, founded in 1152

27 Richmond from the castle. Holy Trinity Church, at the centre of the great cobbled market square, is the regimental museum of the Green Howards

Even now, Wensleydale cheese is not what it was, and what it had been ever since the monks of Jervaulx Abbey first started making it. If you have ever tasted that original Wensleydale cheese you will know what I mean. Offered the choice between 'real' Wensleydale and ambrosia, whatever that might consist of, I would take Wensleydale! Creamy and smooth, it astonishes the palate with a delicacy of flavour almost unbelievable and certainly unlike anything else.

You couldn't make it just anywhere, not even in Wensleydale – only where the land was rich in chalk, from the limestone, which gave the cheese its remarkable whiteness.

The war effectively killed off that very special, ancient cheese because cheese rationing required the introduction of grading. Many a Dales farmer's wife was horrified to find her Wensleydale cheese in third or fourth place because of its high degree of moisture and low acidity – precisely the qualities, of course, which made it 'Wensleydale'.

Rather than make 'fourth-grade' cheese the farmers, whose wives had won prizes for years with their 'Wensleydale', let the Milk Marketing Board send tankers to collect the raw milk – it was a more economical procedure anyway, because there were then no wages to be paid to cheesemakers in the dairy. And that was part of the tragedy, because when rationing ended after the war, not one out of nearly 200 registered 'Wensleydale' makers was prepared to resume manufacture by the traditional method. In any case, it took quite an effort to remember how! And even if they could remember, the introduction of pasteurisation made the old method, if not impossible, illegal . . . which is not to say that it isn't made quietly in remote corners of the Dales.

You can still buy Wensleydale cheese, of course, any day of the week and good cheese it is; but there's another cheese that you can only buy if you know where to find it. That, too, is called Wensleydale and has been for a long, long time.

The girl who served my dinner said she was going to the tup sales at Hawes next day. The ewes had been on sale today, she said, but it was the tups that fetched the big money, 'five or six thousand pounds, sometimes', she said, understandably impressed.

'I shouldn't want something that had cost me that much much money roaming about on the moors'. And at the mercy, she could have added, of any hare-brained motorist (may literate hares forgive me) who cannot suit his speed to his situation.

The danger time is just after lambing, when the delightfully footloose lambs gambol in the sunshine, blissfully lacking the road sense, sometimes painfully acquired, of their elders. Nature, unfortunately, seems never to have equipped sheep with the means of warning their young of such unnatural hazards as motorists. So what *do* you do if you hit a sheep?

Tell the police at the first call box you come to, and if an injury needs attention, as it probably will, look up the nearest R.S.P.C.A. inspector's number as well.

It isn't necessary for you to determine who owns the animal. That's a specialist job which would require you to possess a copy of *The Shepherd's Guide* in which are listed the horn burn marks, earclippings and brand, rud or paint marks on the fleece that show on which farm the sheep was reared.

At the tup show next day, the animals were in no danger from me! A woolly bullet hurtled from the sale ring and almost knocked me down. Unwisely, I was standing near the entrance, the sale ring itself being crammed with a veritable expertise of Swaledale fanciers. The tup was seized by the thick fleece and thrust without ceremony into a pen, the rails of which he promptly jumped to join other aristocrats in sympathetic nose licking. He was a fine, big animal with a head which made me realise how well chosen is the emblem of the Yorkshire Dales National Park. His white-nosed facial markings were clearly defined, and I remembered that my informant of the previous evening had said that a sheep farmer friend 'washes their noses with Daz!'

I wondered how many of the shepherds and farmers present still counted their sheep by the traditional method. Not one, two and three, but *yan, tyan tethera*: then *methera pip, ceser* (four, five, six) and so on. Ten becomes *dick*, eleven is *yanadick* and twelve *tyanadick*. Fifteen is rather endearingly replaced by *bumpit*, sixteen is *manabumpit* (one and fifteen); seventeen becomes *tyanabumpit*, eighteen *tetherabumpit*, nineteen *methera-bumpit* and so to twenty, or *jiggit*. And all, of course, with local variations, such as *mymph* for fifteen and the omission, sometimes, of *tetheradick* (thirteen) for the usual reason.

Where did it come from, this practice of counting to ten, then to 15, then starting again at 15 and one? It is shared with Welsh-speakers, though the terms are reputedly much older than the medieval Welsh drovers, who are said to have employed the method while rustling cattle on the English border – counting in fives with the fingers of one hand, whilst in the other they held a stout cudgel! One way to count to a hundred without benefit of computer or calculator is to raise one finger each time you reach 20. Five fingers up equals one hundred. Put a pebble in your pocket and start again.

Well over 100,000 sheep and lambs and 12,000 cattle are auctioned every year at Hawes, a figure well in excess of its present human population of around 1,200.

For centuries rope-making has been one of the traditional Wensley-dale crafts, exemplified in our own time by Tom Outhwaite, of Hawes, who continued the business of his father. Only a few years ago magazine articles described Tom as 'Yorkshire's last craftsman ropemaker' and dilated on his apparently insoluble problem of finding someone to succeed him in the long, low wooden shed where he had practised skills learned over many years.

Then, one day, Ruth Annison called at the rope works and, fascinated as so many other visitors have been, watched Tom at his work. When, in conversation, the rope-maker disclosed that he would be glad to sell the business when he retired, it started the train of events which led to Ruth and her husband taking over that business in 1975. As a textile chemist, Dr Peter Annison already had a good knowledge of the raw materials and some understanding of the processes involved.

But in many ways the business must have appeared to be an anachronism. The rope yarns are warped by hand between the hooks on the twisting machine and the hook on what, from its appearance, is called a 'sledge'; and are twisted to form the strands for a rope. By means of a grooved cone called a 'top' the strands are laid together into a rope. At first sight it would appear unlikely that making each rope individually by hand could be competitive in today's world.

In fact the business has expanded rapidly. More staff are now employed and new machinery has been installed. The traditional products of Tom's day, halters and cow ties, are still made, but to these has been added a range of lead ropes, horse haynets and wagon ropes for agricultural use. A wide range of rope- and twine-based craft items has been developed, too, including macramé plant hangers, hammocks, dog leads, rope dolls, skipping ropes, quoits. Recent developments include church bell ropes with the coloured wool sallies, ship's fenders and decorative bannister and barrier ropes.

A good example of an old industry very much alive and thriving, using traditional methods but adapting these where appropriate to give greater productivity and so ensure that Hawes still has its ropemaker.

South of Hawes, and almost a part of it, is Gayle. It is said that once there was a keen rivalry between the two places. If so, it has long been forgotten and Gayle has slipped out of the race into a comfortable retirement. The Gayle Beck, with its series of waterfalls, notably Gayle Force and Aisgill Force, divides the village, a place of odd nooks and corners dating back as a place of human habitation to those early Celtic Dalesmen who left their calling cards in the shape of flint arrow-heads and such.

Parking or camping on Gayle Green, let me warn you, is prohibited, but you'll hardly be tempted to the latter transgression since the 'Green' is all asphalt and concrete. But it makes a good vantage point from which to view some of my favourite Gayle residents – the ducks. With their companions, the geese, they besiege your car (not parked on the green, I hope) and the long-necked white members of the deputation reach up and peck imperiously at your window. Be warned: take some bread with you when you visit Gayle or be prepared to come away feeling like a criminal.

A local man, tossing bread to them from the bridge, told me of the rather surprising origins of the ducks of Gayle. They came to the Dales as a sitting of eggs from, of all places, Blackpool. Their ultimate purpose was to be shot at, but the ducks apparently had other ideas. As my Gayle friend put it, 'You couldn't shoot 'em now – they're too tame!' Visitors come from miles around, he said, to see Gayle's sitting ducks which became sitting tenants.

North-west of Hawes, at Hardraw, the Green Dragon Inn gives access not only to Hardraw Force, at one hundred feet the highest single-drop waterfall in England, but to the natural limestone amphitheatre which in recent years has been the scene of a remarkable revival.

Many years ago Hardraw was famous in the Dales and attracted the holders of no less famous names from wider spheres – for instance the great Blondin, who stopped to cook a nonchalant omelette while crossing its impressive chasm by tightrope. Its fame was greatest, however, amongst the 'banding' fraternity. From 1881 to 1929 they made the limestone walls of the gorge echo their ringing arpeggios at band contests before audiences who packed the natural terraces fashioned into rough stone seats.

Great reputations were made at Hardraw in those days. The renowned Black Dyke Mills Band found early fame here at a time when these competitions were considered second only to those held at the Crystal Palace – to which, indeed, success at Hardraw might well prove a final stepping stone. So great was the attraction that as many as 26 special train-loads of harmony addicts would steam into Hawes and, when their trains had been parked in down-dale sidings, would walk to Hardraw via Charcoal Fields, where lame and blind beggars would line the route with outstretched hands. No doubt the pickings were often good, for at the height of their fame, the 'Brass Band and Glee Contests' could attract 18,000 visitors.

Nor were the beggars the only ones to recognise a good opportunity. . . . In 1894 glasses of water were sold to the (largely Yorkshire) crowds for one penny each! It *must* have been hot. . . . And how the bandsmen must have sweated during the customary march through Hawes (before the contest proper) to be judged at the Fountain Hotel on the smartness of their turn-out.

A treasured poster announcing the event of 1885 offers prizes to the value of £42 for bands and £17 for glee singing. There was to be dancing, too, and near the foot of the bill reference is made, almost as an afterthought, to Hardraw's 'Magnificent Waterfall'. Admission then cost one shilling. The very lowest item on that poster of 1885 might be considered in a way prophetic. It is headed 'Excursion Trains'. . . .

Year by year, Hardraw rang to the music of the bandsmen, sometimes uniformed, often bowler-hatted, usually bewhiskered. Then, in 1929 (I don't know why), it stopped. The deep, narrow valley fell silent, the stone terrace seats became overgrown, lichen grew on the circular stone bandstand, which remained to puzzle visitors who wondered if they had come across a new kind of 'stone circle'.

I wish I could say that it was a Yorkshire band that revived this hallowed custom after nearly 50 years of neglect, but in fact the impetus came – and all honour to them – from the Kirkby Lonsdale Band. But bands in the Dales (as well as in Lancashire and what is now called Cumbria) were quick to join in when it was proposed in 1976 to revive the contests.

British Rail, too, played its part, allowing passengers to alight – for the first time in who knows how long – at Garsdale, the once-renowned 'Hawes junction', one of the remotest stations, even in the Dales. (Garsdale, I must tell you, is rich in railway horror stories. You hear of the locomotive spun around while standing on a turntable by the unaided force of the wind alone; of engines funnel-high in snow. And, long before the railways came, it was at Garsdale in 1615 that the hundred householders were said to be unable to travel to church in winter without risking their lives.)

So once again, in 1976, the silvery notes of cornets filled the air, demonstrating that those bandsmen of 50 years ago knew a thing or two about acoustics, while at the other end of the valley, only yards wide at its deepest point, Hardraw Force poured endlessly over its rocky lip – as it always does, except when ice sculpts the falling stream into fantastic white pillars. (Not that everyone is invariably impressed by the torrent: I think it was a Bradford man, who said he could see nowt to 'od it back.)

Again in 1977 and 1978 a band contest was held at Hardraw, and there seems every reason to hope that the harmonious tradition is now thoroughly re-established, even if the 'gate' does not always equal the 18,000 of bygone times.

Of the ways from Wensleydale to Swaledale, the best known is the Buttertubs Pass, which starts near Hardraw and soars past hummocky Abbotside Common on its way to Thwaite. The views here make you catch your breath. On the right, a little way before the 'tubs' themselves is Lovely Seat (2,213 feet), whilst Great Shunner Fell rises 2,340 feet just a few miles to the west.

Two or three miles before reaching Thwaite and Swaledale you find the far-famed Buttertubs themselves. Geologists, no doubt, can say how these limestone cavities were formed. Perhaps the mixture of rainwater and carbon dioxide, which I am told can dissolve limestone, caused these striking, fissures, fluted like outsize organ pipes, in the body of the fell. Not really dangerous, except perhaps to young children or over-enthusiastic dogs: at the same time, not to be treated with disrespect – depths vary from 50 to 100 feet, or as the old Dalesman said when questioned on this very point, 'Why, noo, yer askin' me summat! But they do tell me some of 'em's bottomless – or 'appen even deeper!'

To the east, far below, Cliff Beck flashes in the sun as it twists and turns. Ahead is Kisdon Hill (1,636 feet). Thwaite is on the left and its twin village, Muker, reclines comfortably on the right at Kisdon's feet.

That as I say, is the popular way to reach Swaledale, but I prefer the wilder, lonelier road from Askrigg, where grouse are commoner that tourists and Oxnop Scar rears as a long wall of outcropping limestone which is to me at least as impressive as the Buttertubs. Another road from Askrigg branches out just beyond the village to take a longer more easterly route to Swaledale, crossing Whitaside Moor to Grinton.

A few miles south-west of Hardraw in the huddled hamlet of Appersett. Still further along the westward road, not far past little Cotter Force, lovely in spring with primroses, is Cotterdale – another of the half-hidden 'little dales' branching from the main dale. A signpost reading 'Cotterdale Only' points into the past.

Three Halls, two Kirks and a King,
Same road out as goes in.

That is how a bygone rhymester described Cotterdale – Hall, Kirk and King were the names of the families who lived there. Probably there are no more people in Cotterdale now than were there then – and many of those are in the little Methodist burial ground.

One of its gravestones – nobody knows whose – reads 'We repose in peace here', and if you point out to a Cotterdale man that there is no name or date on the stone you might well receive the traditional reply: 'We know who they are'.

Beside the former chapel, so like a barn, Shepherd's Cottage bears the date 1616. There are few other houses, now, though a hundred years and more ago there were possibly 30. But that was in the time when coal was mined here from seams running beneath Great Shunner Fell.

It seems hard to believe today that such a sweetly pastoral place could ever have been associated with such a grimy industry, but this kind of coal-mining had little in common with towering pit stacks and black, louring spoil heaps. The methods used were even more primitive, perhaps, than those used in the old lead-mines of Swaledale. Until the early years of this century, the Cotterdale miners drove their galleries 500 yards or more into the fell-side. By the light of candles, in tunnels no wider than the three-foot seams they are working, the Cotterdale men loaded their hard-won coal into wheeled trolleys which were then hauled by man-power to larger wagons waiting in the galleries. The Pennine Way, beloved of venturesome and energetic walkers, passes plenty of disused pits on its way north, and you may reach the Way from Cotterdale by one of the very tracks the miners made.

Not all the dead who died in Cotterdale were Methodists. Anglicans, too, found rest in the lonely graveyard, set amid fields and fells and plantations, at Lunds, reached by the path to Shaws Youth Hostel. The little church here would seat perhaps 50 at a squeeze; the benches, hardly wide enough to accommodate modern posteriors, are redolent of furniture polish and loving care. It was a different scene that William Howitt found in 1839. The roof was holed and as there was no bell, the clerk did his best (almost literally) to fill the breach by intoning 'bol-bol' with his head through the roof.

Lunds, with its broad churchyard of sometimes fallen, usually unreadable gravestones, its mist-enveloped silence, is a melancholy place, with a sadness which must have entered the souls of its bygone residents. At least one of its priests thought so. Since his arrival, he said, there had been neither wedding nor funeral at Lunds, sure proof, in his view that his flock had no more love for each other than God had for them!

SIX

Swaledale to Teesdale

A Diversity of Treasures

Richmond, by the swift-flowing Swale, is possibly the best-loved town in Yorkshire. Proof of the affection it has inspired for centuries may surely be found in the existence of a multitude of Richmonds throughout the world. Though the *Guinness Book of Records* records 43, another investigator claims that the total of Richmonds – cities, towns and villages – is at least 54.

Southerners, in that superior way of theirs, will no doubt claim that the original of them all was Richmond, Surrey, just as they lay claim even to the Sweet Lass of Richmond Hill herself, an unimpeachably Yorkshire lady, as I hope to establish.

To be fair, perhaps a few – *just* a few of those overseas Richmonds take their name from the one in Surrey, but you won't convince an informed Yorkshireman, of that; he being well aware that the Richmond on the Thames, originally called Sheen, was re-named in honour of Richmond on the Swale by Henry VII (who was Earl of Richmond, Yorkshire) when he rebuilt the Palace of Sheen.

It seems rather a glaring example of southern bias that some encyclopaedias mention the earlier Richmond only in connection with the later one, which, though the site of a Royal residence from the twelfth century onwards and now the home no doubt of a bigger population than Yorkshire's Richmond, can scarcely be more interesting.

With its Arthurian legend, its Georgian Theatre, its enormous cobbled market place surrounding the twelfth-century church of Holy Trinity (now the regimental Museum of the Green Howards, 'Family Regiment' of the North Riding), Richmond is the one town I might make compulsory on visitors' itineraries – had I the power or the inclination.

Start with the castle, since it is the oldest and certainly the most awesome structure in the town (witness the inevitable artists trying to reduce the soaring keep, a hundred and more feet high, to a size they can hang on the wall). This is said to be the oldest stone castle in England, founded in 1071 by the Norman Alan Rufus, whose object in building it is hardly as clear as the turbulent waters of the Swale washing its feet on the southern side.

Away up in Swaledale, Red Alan was hardly likely to be involved in any major battles. Possibly the castle's enormous strength in a setting where there was little likelihood of fighting – apart from an occasional skirmish with the Scots – is a mark of the respect in which the Norman conquerors held the men whose homes and lands they had commandeered.

As we entered by the barbican we fell in behind a school party led by a teacher who had done at least as much homework as his class. . . . 'This gateway is modern, of course – now keep together, I don't want to be rounding you up again, like a flock of Swaledale sheep' – a burst of laughter – because even with a teacher's jokes, touring a castle in the sunshine is better than algebra any April day.

'We keep left – *left* – and follow the curtain wall to the Robin Hood tower. Now here, according to tradition, William the Lion, King of Scotland, was imprisoned after his defeat at the Battle of Alnwick in 1174. *Don't* be ridiculous, he was called the Lion because of his bravery. . . .'

At the tiny Chapel of St Nicholas the class was duly instructed on the semi-circular arches and shafts, of the wall arcade, with their simple capitals. . . . 'And now, here we are in Scolland's Hall, a very fine example of period architecture. . . . Now we go back to the Great Court . . . Turn right – *right* – and down the steps. *No* pushing, *please*! And turn left at the bottom. Now we're in the Cockpit, measuring 220 feet from east to west and 170 feet north to south, where jousting used to take place. You can almost imagine the ladies looking down on the knights from the towers there. . . .'

I wondered if these ladies also spared a glance now and then for the Swale, which must have looked much the same as it does now. Or were their eyes so accustomed to natural beauty that they preferred to admire the armoured figures competing for their attention in what is now a pleasant garden, where children's voices are heard instead of martial cries and the clash of weapons on armour?

'On your left', said the teacher is the Gold Hole Tower. . . .

Some day, when I have no more books to write I shall find the passage beneath the tower that leads to King Arthur's treasure, and thus ensure for myself a prosperous old age. Or at least, I would if I could find Potter Thompson, who discovered those same riches many years ago. I would love to ask him how it all happened and I have no doubt that he would be delighted to tell it all, for the hundredth time, in pure North Riding, the most musical of Yorkshire dialects (here reproduced as best a West Riding man can).

'Why, noo, it wor like this. Ah was walkin' aboot the castle when Ah saw this tunnel. Ah deean't know why, bud Ah'd niver noaticed it afooar. An' Ah deean't knaw ti this day what made mi go inside. There seemed ti be summat *drawin' me in*, as ye might say, an' it wor just as if mi feet adn't got a mind o' their own!

'Doon an' doon, deeper under the castle Ah went, alang tunnels an' passages Ah'd niver knawn wor theer. Then, ahl at once Ah turned a corner an' theer they wor – King Arthur an' his knights snorin' fit to bust! Ah wor a'most freetened to deeath, Ah con tell thi.

'Then Ah saw this gre't kist, an' a sword, an' a gre't horn, bigger nor Ah ivver saw affooar. That sword! Ah'd niver seen owt so grand in mi life. A'most affooar Ah knew it, Ah'd stretched oot mi hand ti draw it frav its scabbard. Then Ah 'eard a sooart o' sigh. It wor King Arthur stirrin' in his sleep! If Ah'd been freetened affooar, Ah wor terrified noo! Whatever wod King Arthur say if he wakkened up an' fun' me tryin' ter pinch his sword? Then he spok', an' Ah a'most fell deead . . . "Is it time?" he said, stretchin'. 'E meant, thoo sees, is it time for me ti wakken an' save England. But Ah thowt, No, it's time for me ti be off! Ah turned roond an' withoot a backward look Ah ran fra' that cave as if all the fiends of 'ell wor at mi 'eels . . .

'It wor then Ah 'eard it – that voice . . . it seemed to echo through the cave, all 'ollow an' ghostly:

> *Potter, Potter Thompson,*
> *If thou hadst either drawn the sword*
> *Or blown the horn:*
> *Thou'd been the luckiest man*
> *That ever yet was born*

'Aye 'appen, Ah thowt! Ah wor more consarned, thoo sees, ti get away wi mi life. Ah suppose Ah missed mi chance, an' it niver did coom ageean, for Ah could niver ageean find that tunnel under t'castle – no matter 'ow Ah tried! Worst of it was, there wor them 'at wouldn't believe it 'ad ivver 'appened at all!'

Sleep soundly, Potter Thompson, wherever you are. *I* believe you . . . well, almost. After all, I myself have met a king in Richmond – or at least, our visits coincided, even if I was more aware of him than he was of me. That king was Olav of Norway, Colonel-in-Chief of the Green Howards, who opened the regiment's museum in the old, redundant Church of Holy Trinity in the market square, a twelfth-century structure long noted, among other reasons, for the fact that shops and a café were built into its walls.

The Church Commissioners offered the old church to the Green Howards for a peppercorn rent and £90,000 was spent in adapting it to its new rôle. You may wonder why the King of Norway should be colonel-in-chief of a North Riding infantry regiment. The answer takes us back over a century to when Princess Alexandra, one of his ancestors, was herself accorded that rank after presenting new colours in 1875. Two years before, the Green Howards (Nineteenth Regiment of Foot) began their association with the town which still contains their headquarters, as well as the museum, which is one of the finest of its type in Yorkshire.

Richmond has been a soldiers' town for about a thousand years, but especially so since 1925 when Catterick Camp, virtually a town in itself, began, just a few miles away, providing employment and increased prosperity for the town for whom the sight of regimental ceremonial, as when, for instance, the Royal Signals march through annually with colours flying, is a source of familiar pride. Or it might be the R.A.F. Regiment for, like the Signals, and the Green Howards, 'R.A.F. Catterick' holds the Freedom of Richmond.

And still we have things to see in the castle.

We parted from our scholastic friends thankful that we didn't have to write an essay for a teacher's inspection next week; glad, too, that we could amble aimlessly at will, climbing to the top of that square, apparently indestructible tower, which was added above the castle gatehouse in the thirteenth century – an afterthought which now overshadows, in every sense, the original conception of the castle and the town which has grown about its feet and on which I am always fascinated to look down. On that day there were market stalls and all the cheerful bustle of country shopping on the cobbles surrounding the church and the obelisk.

Return (as guidebooks say) to the tower in the south-west corner of the Great Court and I find myself wondering why it seems so surprising that Lord Baden Powell, the 'B.P.', venerated in my Boy Scout days, is commemorated here by a plaque. Apparently he was 'stationed' in the castle at some time during his career and it was here that he made some of his early sketches for his book *Scouting for Boys*. No doubt he was a far more willing guest than some others who, though they lacked either the fame or the martial spirit of B.P., left their own touching marks on the castle where few visitors have seen them. They were Conscientious Objectors, imprisoned here during the war of 1914–18.

A mixed bag, those 'prisoners of conscience'. They were locked up in eight cells which once formed part of the guardroom of the barracks built in the castle grounds sometime around the middle of the last century. Some were Communists, some Quakers (and some, perhaps, just plain awkward) and the walls of the old cell block bear witness to their variety, besides at least 50 of their names.

As prisoners always do, they passed the weary hours by writing and drawing on the walls. They wrote the words of the Red Flag or of hymns whose poignancy echoed their own sense of martyrdom. And one, perhaps disenchanted with the high-minded views which had brought him to this state of misery, inscribed the music of *Home Sweet Home*! upon the wall.

One, who might be a character in a play by Shaw, writes: 'The only War which is worth fighting is the Class War. The Working Class of this Country have no quarrel with the Working Class of Germany or any other Country. Socialism stands for Internationalism. If the workers of all countries united and refused to fight, there would be no war'. One prisoner drew a picture of Christ, fallen beneath the weight of the cross and beneath it wrote:

> *Every cross grows light beneath*
> *The shadow, Lord, of Thine.*

'I was brought up from Pontefract', wrote one man, with a suggestion of outraged simplicity, 'on Friday, August 11th, 1916, and put in this cell for refusing to become a soldier'. One feels he was striving to convince himself that such a thing could happen. Another drew a picture of a girl with pinned-back hair in the style of 1916 and wistfully captioned it 'My Kathleen'.

Again and again the date 1916 appears, for this was the year the Military Service Act, introduced by the Morley-born Prime Minister, Asquith, was passed. Perhaps because there was too little space for them in the civil prisons, some of the despised 'conchies' were held temporarily at Richmond, and just as surely imprisoned as if at Strangeways or Brixton. Their food was passed to them through tiny hatches and the wardens watched them narrowly through spy holes. The cells are said to have been damp and cold and the sanitary arrangements deplorable.

It is said that 40 such, 17 of them from Richmond, were ordered to join the colours in France, but they refused to be soldiers and were sentenced to death, only to be reprieved. And there is a story – perhaps it is nothing more – that on the journey south the unwilling warriors threw from the train a note describing their situation and that this note reached the House of Commons.

What a relief to turn from such sombre matters to Richmond's Georgian gem of a theatre, where we sat grandly, in one of the boxes emblazoned with the names of bygone dramatists, which surround the miniature auditorium. The next box bore the name of one of the wittiest of English writers, Congreve, born at Bardsey, near Leeds, while that opposite commemorated his contemporary competitor Sir John Vanbrugh, whose many-sided genius produced, among much else, the magnificence of Castle Howard, near York.

How apt that this magical little theatre, built in 1788 and the only one of that period surviving in its original form, should have been discovered at Richmond.

You enter the theatre from Friar's Wynd (pronounced *weend*) by a small door that you might easily miss were it not for the sign above reading 'Georgian Theatre'. Ivor Brown said the grey stone building looked like 'a barn that had come to town' – and so it does. A grey stone barn whose entrance might lead anywhere but on to the world contained within. We hear much of the cliché about 'stepping into a bygone age'; but if it is true anywhere it is true here!

Hardly changed is the tiny paybox or the narrow flight of stone steps by which you may reach the boxes named after Shakespeare, Johnson, Farquhar, Goldsmith, Sheridan, Rowe, Dryden. Past the boxes, the steps lead up to the gallery where the original barracking board, kicked by Georgian feet nearly two centuries ago, remains in place for present-day audiences too polite to use it. From the stepped pit every member of the audience has a good view of the beautiful little stage, whose red curtains match the canvas at the rear of the boxes: the looped drop curtains are a soft green, in the Georgian style, like the panels and doors.

Richmond was not unknown to the theatrical fraternity even before it had a theatre. In the old days, strolling players would give resounding performances from an extensive repertoire whenever there was a barn or a hall they could use. Then one Samuel Butler, who had been running the Theatre Royal in York, came to Richmond, to ask the Corporation's permission to build 'a proper theatre' there. With commendable foresight they said he could, and they offered him the site at the junction of Friar's Wynd and Victoria Road, where the theatre stands to this day.

Samuel was clearly confident that his success would enable him to meet the yearly rent of £5, plus taxes, which his venture would cost. So he built his theatre and it was duly opened on 2 September, 1788. The audience, goodness knows how, numbered 400: today a capacity house is considered to total no more than 238: but doubtless we are larger, or more demanding of elbow room today.

During succeeding decades, Richmond was regaled with everything from Shakespeare and comic opera to a tightrope walker whose aerial path took him from stage to gallery – and he nonchalantly wheeling a barrow the while! Offering such delights you might think it could hardly fail to enthral the folk of Richmond, but fail it did, though the stage was trodden for 40 years after Samuel died.

Then the theatre came down in the world – with an almost theatrical bump! It became a corn store, then a furniture store, part of it served as a wine cellar, and in 1940, or thereabouts, it was 'called up' for use as a wartime salvage store – and that, suprisingly was the making of the Georgian Theatre as we see it today.

Everyone knew it had been a theatre, but not until its 'discovery' in 1940 was its truly *Georgian* character established, in that it had a stepped pit and raised stage; but these it certainly had, though the wine cellar had until then effectively disguised the existence of the pit.

Strong evidence was provided by three nailed-down trap doors found on what had been the stage – clearly the actors who appeared or disappeared through them must have had somewhere to go *to* and come *from*, between their sudden exits and entrances; and clearly they could not have reached the place by penetrating the wine cellar roof! The only way to find out for certain would be to demolish the wine cellar, but what if that resulted in the unintended demolition of the theatre itself? The then Town Clerk of Richmond, David Brooks, decided that the risk was one worth taking and so the lovely little theatre gradually reappeared in all its Georgian splendour – raised stage, stepped pit, boxes, seats and all.

And in May 1963 the theatre was reopened with a gala performance graced by the two theatrical Grand Dames Edith Evans and Sybil Thorndike, the latter having accepted the presidency of the Richmond Theatre Trust on condition that the theatre stayed 'live'. And live it has certainly stayed. Names as illustrious as those of Butler's time and of the Keans and Trees of their day now grace its playbills during its annual summer season, and even those unknown outside the Women's Institute can often command an audience in this enchanted setting.

Richmond never ceases to surprise me by the 'suitability' of what I discover there. Só Lewis Caroll was once a pupil (as C.L. Dodgson, his real name) at the grammar school. Well, what more natural? Nor must we forget the most romantic denizen of all, the Sweet Lass herself, Frances I'Anson, who lived at Hill House opposite the top of French-gate. The 'lass more bright than Mayday morn' was beloved by Leonard McNally, an Irish barrister who wrote the song and in 1787 married its inspiration. It was an immediate success at Vauxhall and Covent Garden because the public thought it referred to Mrs Fitz-herbert, morganatic wife of the Prince Regent. Frances died before she was 30, but with her brother, then mayor of the town, she attended the opening of the theatre in 1788 – not dreaming that nearly two hundred years later a song about her would be sung at the theatre's re-opening.

If I could write fairy tales I would make Richmond my setting for most of them, for there is surely a fairy tale quality about customs like the ringing of the 'Prentice Bell', morning and evening from the clock tower of the old Holy Trinity Church at the centre of the market cobbles, and of the Pancake Bell on Shrove Tuesday. And still I have not mentioned the medieval Grey Friars Tower, or another elegant tower commemor-ating the victory at Culloden – and so much else that I despair of doing justice to Richmond in anything less than a whole book.

'I am Swedish. Can you tell me where is the pub? In Sweden we drink very much.' I directed him as requested 'Such hills!' said the Swede, as if Sweden were some kind of table-land. 'It is easier to go down than up! . . . I hope I have not inconvenienced you.'

He hadn't, of course. If I had nothing else to do I could gladly spend my time directing entertaining foreigners to Richmond pubs. And there have been plenty to direct, both before and since the British Council chose Richmond as their example of a typical country town. If only it were! Ideal, yes. Typical, alas, no.

Richmond has changed little, I am glad to say, since the time about 15 years ago, when I wrote in a magazine: 'Richmond . . . is a living town . . . with an amazing variety of customs which still mean something in the life of its people. On the day when the Mayor receives the "First Fruits" of the new season's wheat, in the Market Square, and does it chiefly for the diversion of tourists, the ceremony will have as little significance as the dances performed by present-day American Indians for the amusement of gawping palefaces.'

And I still believe, as I did then, that to save its civic soul in the face of touristy temptation, Richmond 'ought to make Potter Thompson its patron saint – he may have missed a fortune, but at least he lived to tell the tale'.

I am able to drag myself away from Richmond partly because my next destination is so pleasantly reached. For Easby Church, with its thirteenth century frescoes, and the neighbouring abbey ruins are only a mile to the south-east along a winding riverside path. The ruins are the most extensive of any Premonstratensian abbey in the Dales, founded in 1152 by a Constable of Richmond named Roaldus and dedicated to St Agatha of Sicily, famous (as you may read in the church porch) for her gentleness and beauty. The church was founded before the abbey, and its walls are adorned with paintings representing the seasons and depicting Man's Fall and restoration through the ministry and death of Christ.

That is as far as we go to the east. The old road westward from Richmond to Reeth, passing through Marske, offers superb views of the town and its castle, while on the right, Beacon Hill rises over a thousand feet above sea level. This was the eminence on which sentries at the castle must keep their eyes; for a red glow in the sky meant danger – perhaps of invasion.

There was no such kindly warning for Robert Willance. In 1606 he was hunting in these parts when a thick fog came down and Robert's horse blundered blindly over the edge of the 200-foot Whitcliffe Scar! Robert escaped with his life, though his horse was killed and both his own legs were broken. He knew that on such a night he had little chance of being quickly found – and that if he were *not* found, the cold alone would kill him. So he cut open the body of his horse and sheltered inside it until help came. The plan born of desperation worked – Robert lived: all of him, that is, except one leg which found a premature resting place in the churchyard, there to await the rest of Robert, which joined it not ten years after.

To this day the spot is called Willance's Leap – though the word 'flight' might be more appropriate. Not that it did him much permanent harm. He prospered and became an alderman of Richmond – if a one-legged one. A monument marks the site of his leap, but the most prized memento of his deliverance is the silver chalice he presented to the town.

Marske is sometimes confused with Marske-by-the-Sea, still in North Yorkshire to the Yorkshireman (though the 'reorganisers' would claim that Cleveland is now a separate county). The two places have little else in common: Marske-by-the-Sea is a fisherman's town, whereas Marske in Swaledale is the sort of place where a sailor sick of the sea might seek to settle – for there, if anywhere, they might really ask him the purpose of the oar he carried on his shoulder!

Marske has a fine old church with Norman features, as well as box pews rare in Dales churches. And Marske Hall, here, was once the home of a family named Halton, who in 1599 provided a primate of England and in 1757 a Primate of All England (in other words an Archbishop of York and one of Canterbury in that order). South-west of the village a 60-foot obelisk bears witness to the love of Captain Matthew Hutton for this part of Swaledale. In accordance with his will he was buried on this spot when he died here in 1814.

At Reeth, in the former Methodist Sunday School near the green, there is one of the most attractive small folk museums I have seen – no mere collection of locally gathered bygones but an attempt to show the life of Swaledale and Arkengarthdale in days gone by.

The explanations attached to the exhibits are themselves an introduction to Dales life and custom: 'Except for raids by Romans, Vikings and the Scots, national history more or less passed Swaledale by. It was never on the road to anywhere in particular. Roads were poor . . . . Only those with farming or lead-mining connections lived here permanently, so very little was written down of life as it happened.' Which is partly what makes museums like this so fascinating today.

Here is much information about the old lead-mining days which ended about a century ago, when, incidentally, the miners and farmers who lived there were still rejoicing in the comparatively new-found blessing of water, no longer obtainable only from springs, but from taps on the large green: and all thanks to George Robinson, who lived there, and who, being one of the 'big house' fraternity, had the means to provide a tank for the collection of water half a mile to the north.

Grinton, a little way south-east of Reeth, is where Reeth folk go to church, for the parish which centres on the lovely church is huge and at one time reached out to touch Westmorland (now part of the 'new county' of 'Cumbria').

Like the church at Romaldkirk in Teesdale, it is called, 'the Cathedral of the Dales'. And with at least as good a claim, for this large and venerably beautiful church with its Norman features, its 'lepers' squint', its scratches probably made by arrow-sharpeners waiting for their masters to end their worship, was the destination for travellers on the 'Corpse Way'.

For a brief explanation, return to that splendid folk museum at Reeth, where you may read: 'Prior to 1580 people who died "up-dale" and who wished to be buried in consecrated ground were carried in wicker baskets along the Corpse Way to Grinton. The road from Keld via Ivelet Bridge can still be walked and stones seen which are said to be resting places for the coffins. The journey must have taken two days (or more in bad weather). . . . Even after Muker churchyard was in use, bodies had to be carried long distances. Above Feetham (Low Row) are remains of a building known as the "dead house", where the bodies were left while the bearers refreshed themselves at the Punch Bowl Inn.'

We, too, in due time, will call at the Punch Bowl Inn, but our present route leads in the opposite direction – back to Richmond on the lovely riverside road that takes us between Marrick and Ellerton Priories, only a mile apart across the Swale.

Marrick, founded as a nunnery by Roger de Aske in the time of King Stephen, is a 'mixed community' today, though the youthful inhabitants of the hostel built into the priory shell are clearly neither monks nor nuns. Still with a religious inspiration, it has been called a 'kind of spiritual Outward Bound Centre'.

There is certainly an element of adventure in getting there if you take the steps – originally one for each day of the year – which have probably existed since black-robed Benedictine nuns descended them after a walk through the woods from the village. In their time, however, the steps would be less hazardous, because less slippery from moss and moisture; less broken by age, too, in those far-off days described by Hilda F.M. Prescott in *The Man on a Donkey*.

Ellerton Priory, south of the Swale and about a mile downstream, was dissolved at about the same time, over four hundred years ago. It was founded in the reign of Henry II. It is unlikely, by the way, to find a new purpose in the manner of Marrick, for no shell remains that once enclosed its cloisters – only a single, lonely tower.

Passing close to Downholme and Hudswell, the road winds to Richmond. At Downholme the ghost of Mary Stuart is said to haunt nearby Walburn Hall, where the sad queen occupied an upper room during a 'holiday' – if such it can be called – from the sterner prison of Bolton Castle in Wensleydale. East of Walburn lie Scotton and the sprawl of Catterick Camp – which takes us back to Richmond.

The principal roads westward from Richmond describe a drunken, sideways figure 8, with Richmond at the 'top' of the figure and Reeth at the middle crossing. Having just completed one loop (the easterly one) of the 'eight', we return to Reeth to make the westerly circuit – to Tan Hill by way of Arkengarthdale, then back to Reeth via Keld, Thwaite, Muker, Gunnerside, Feetham and Healaugh, names with a northern music which conjures the ghosts of Norsemen who left off sea-roving to settle here. The name Arkengarthdale itself is derived from the Old Norse meaning 'the valley of Arkill's enclosure'. Through this, one of the 'little dales' where the real charm of North Yorkshire resides, runs the Arkle Beck from the bleak wastes of Stainmore Forest.

When my friendly waitress at the Spring End Guest House, near Crackpot, told me, while serving dinner, that she was going to the 'CB' that night to dance to the music of a 'group', she meant the hotel half a mile above Langthwaite. It takes its name from an eighteenth-century lord of the manor and entrepreneur, Charles Bathurst, who developed the Dales lead-mining industry. It began with the Romans and is now as dead as they are. As long ago as 1656, mines were bought here by a Dr Bathhurst, and it was his descendants who formed the C.B. company. All that obviously remains are the ruins of old mining buildings and blocked shafts, though the villages themselves and even the footpaths were created to some extent by the needs of the miners for lead or chert, a whitish hard stone used in making fine china.

Langthwaite, the largest settlement in this little dale, appears from the road to fill the floor of the narrow valley through which flows the Arkle Beck. Cross the beck by the little bridge and you enter what seems almost a stone-built Lilliput. Today, quite a few of the tiny dwellings are for sale, for Langthwaite itself is a product of the lead-mining boom now long past. Viking settlers must have named Langthwaite – (its name means 'a long meadow cleared from scrubland'), but it reached its zenith in the nineteenth century and the paths which cross the moors hereabouts were largely made by their heavy-booted feet as they trudged from these little houses to their toil at the mines – and toil, indeed, it was.

But hard as life was for the nineteenth-century Dales lead-miner, it was harder for his forerunners, captive Brigantes whom the Romans compelled, along with condemned prisoners and other unfortunates, to drag the valued metal – which could be used for lining coffins or baths and for making water conduits – from the earth in the year 74 A.D. or thereabouts. The Romans, indeed, are credited with instigating the practice of *hushing*, a method of extracting the ore which was practised in

Swaledale until the 1890s and in Arkengarthdale itself until the present century.

Where lead was known or suspected to be, a dam would be made of stones and turf, in a stream near a hill-top. Then the surface of the soil would be broken up with the pick to form a rough channel. When water filled and burst the dam, to rush like a flood downhill, the soil would be washed away and the vein of lead exposed.

Lead-mining had a language of its own. When, for some reason, *hushing* was not practicable, a *level*, or tunnel would be driven into the hillside. The rough ore, mixed with rock, was called *bouse*. Loaded into trucks, it was conveyed on rails from the level and then sorted on the dressing floor. A job, this, for boys and women; they would use flat hammers called *buckers* to crush the ore, which was then further crushed between rollers, driven by water wheels sometimes 30 feet in diameter, before being washed and having the sulphur removed by roasting. Then it was ready for smelting.

During this exploration of Swaledale the subject of lead-mining will recur from time to time, but meanwhile we must continue the journey along Arkengarthdale, for whose rather cumbersome name I can only apologise – though not with any great sincerity.

The names of Arkengarthdale – Booze, Arkle Town, Eskeleth, Whaw have sometimes a comic, sometimes almost a mystical ring. Some may be of Norse origin, though Booze, for obvious reasons the best known, is said to be derived from the Old English *Bower-house* – 'the house by the river bend'.

This is a lofty, lonely land. To the south, as you move north-westwards towards Tan Hill, are the heights of Great Pinseat (1,914 feet) and Rogan's Seat (2,204 feet). . . . But the Yorkshireman's chauvinism receives a nasty jolt when he reaches the Tan Hill Inn, famous, at its elevation of 1,732 feet above sea level, as 'the highest pub in England' – only to find that before he can enter he must now pass a sign reading *County of Durham*! Can this really be happening, he wonders: we all knew these 'reorganisers' had something to answer for, but when it comes to robbing Yorkshire of possibly her most famous pub the thing is getting past a joke!

In the dear, dead days when Yorkshire was unquestionably herself there was no doubt about the locality of Tan Hill: it was in Yorkshire.

I don't *really* believe, despite appearances, that the boundary sign was erected by a bunch of Durham chaps bent on pulling a fast one on an unquestionably superior neighbour! All the same, it does look suspicious to suspicious minds like mine, and one of these dark nights I might enlist a party of handy looking Tykes from inside the white walls of the pub. We will then uproot that infuriating DURHAM sign and replant it on the other side of this hostelry which has been part of Yorkshire for perhaps 400 years – drunk in by coal-miners who worked the Tan Hill seam, discovered at least as early as the thirteenth century.

Scottish and English drovers, too, travelling on the drovers' trail from Brough to Reeth, ate and drank here. And from the horse fairs of Brough came gipsies to fight and carouse in this setting which suited them so well. Other travellers, who probably found the surroundings less to their taste, were those who from time to time were isolated in these moorland wastes by weeks of snow. In 1963, for instance, Tan Hill was cut off for seven weeks by drifts which at some points were 15 feet deep. Harry Speight, an indefatigable Yorkshire wanderer of an earlier generation, found snow here in June and August 1880, and frost and ice in September.

The inn witnesses scenes of lively and noisy activity at least once a year – in May, when a sheep show, affectionately known as the 'Swaledale Royal' takes place. A great event, this, a gala for breeders and shepherds of those woolly aristocrats of the Swaledale breed. Music from a Dales village band will fill the crisp moorland air and the Tan Hill Inn will do a roaring trade – no matter whether it's in Yorkshire or Durham.

South, now, to Keld, crossing Stonesdale Moor and passing the hamlet named from the narrow valley of West Stonesdale. The name Keld means a place near a river and it was bestowed, as you might guess, by those early Dalesmen, the Vikings. Most of Keld's stone-built cluster lies just off the road at the end of a narrow lane leading from near the erstwhile Cathole Inn, now a filling station. At Keld, houses and farm buildings form a rough circle set amid the fells. Cobbled yards with little gardens lead off the square. And here, in the overgrown burial ground of Keld Chapel (whose sundial, set in the wall, is dated 1840, though the chapel was rebuilt in 1860) sleep the bygone folk of Keld, their resting places marked by weathered stones, sometimes just readable. Alice Scott of Keldside lies here beneath a stone erected 'as a token of affection by her beloved husband'. Poor Alice: she was only 17 when she died on 15 March 1860, but Dales folk were never given to gush.

There is an almost Biblical simplicity about the tablets inside the church (but I should say chapel, for the denomination to which it belongs, is now called United Reformed and was previously, I suppose, Congregational). The plaques commemorate, among others, Edmund Alderson Knowles, of Low Row, who died in 1835 and 'whose interest in Keld chapel led him to give a field on Kisdon, called Broken Intake, as a permanent endowment for its successive ministers'.

Kisdon, 1,636 feet of steep-sided grandeur, is known for its gorge and for Kisdon Force (waterfall). Walkers on the Pennine Way pass this lovely cataract in a woodland setting so peaceful that the most energetic of them will rest from their walking here – or surely nowhere. Closer to Keld is Catrake Force, reached by the good nature of a farmer whose land you must cross to find it. (Watch out for belligerent calves!)

How Edmund Alderson Knowles's gift of 'a field on Kisdon' must have warmed the heart of Edward Stillman, the minister at Keld in those times. He survived Edmund by two years and when he died in 1837 he had served the Dissenters of Keld for 48 years – 'an earnest minister of this chapel. . . . He was a faithful man'. And the name of his wife, who rests with him, 'is held in honour in this dale'.

Stillman was a wandering preacher who came to Keld in 1789 and thereafter, I was not surprised to learn, wandered no more – unless you count the time he walked to London and back, begging £700 on the journey, so that he might enlarge the chapel. Well, he had to raise the money somehow, and his stipend of about £15 a year would hardly run to it – which is why he embarked on what sounds almost like an early 'sponsored walk'.

The chapels of the Dales might tempt a Betjeman from suburban chancels. Two miles to the south, Thwaite chapel stands beside a stream. On the wall, between windows framing a view of the fells, you read verse six of the Twenty-third Psalm – and here you can believe it.

Thwaite is a cluster of cottages, a chapel, a guest house, a gift shop and the bridge that crosses Thwaite Beck as it makes its noisy way from the feet of Great Shunner and its neighbours – High Seat, Rogan's Seat and Lovely Seat, all topping 2,000 feet. The village never lacks visitors, even if permanent inhabitants are few. It is on record in the chapel that 194 folk lived in Thwaite in 1861. What happened to some of them, I wondered, in 1899, when a great storm washed away the chapel's foundations?

In the Sunday school register of those days you might find the names of Cherry and Richard Kearton. The name is perpetuated in Thwaite by the Kearton Guest House, ('speciality ham and eggs'), where splendid views of Kisdon might give you appetite enough to cope with such fare. Here you can learn more of these Keartons, whose names are so warmly remembered, for the lounge contains a bookcase with titles like *At Home with Wild Nature, In the Land of the Lion, Photographing Wild Life Around the World, Wonders of Wild Nature, Cherry Kearton's Travels*; and in every case the author is one of these same Keartons. About one and a half miles south-east, at Muker, there are tablets in the school 'in memory of Cherry and Richard Kearton'.

Born in Thwaite a little over a century ago, they won a fame which must have astonished their fellow villagers, who probably took the animal life of the fields and trees very much for granted and regarded its study as a pastime suitable only for birdnesting boys; something to be put away, with other childish things, on reaching man's estate. Yet in one sense it was birdnesting that set Richard on the course that both their lives followed. For as a boy of seven he fell from a tree and dislocated his hip. The hip was set by a local vet, whose efforts, for some reason, fell so far short of success that thereafter one of the boy's legs was six or eight inches shorter than the other.

It was a handicap with which young Richard soon learned to cope, but to his parents it was a disaster. One night as he lay, supposedly asleep, in the cottage at Thwaite (so small that the whole family slept in one room), he listened to his parents' speculations about their children's future. . . . Jack could find work on a farm, a daughter would become a servant, but what of Richard with his poor lame leg? Surely the future held nowt for him! Listening and weeping, Richard must have vowed that some day he would prove them wrong.

While Richard hobbled the mile to the little school at Muker, his brother sometimes made the journey by penny-farthing. And the exploit was no doubt recalled in his later life as an example of the dash and enterprise he was to show in encounters with lions and rhino. For Cherry became a pioneer of the wild-life photography so many of us revel in as armchair naturalists today.

But these days were still far in the future when Richard set out to walk seven miles along the Buttertubs Pass to Hawes, to catch the train to London and eventual fame as a writer and lecturer on wild life. Cherry, meanwhile, developed as a photographer by illustrating his brother's books.

Richard may well have envied him when Cherry spread his wings to become a world traveller – but not everyone in 'Swardil' approved of such goings-on: like the elderly lady who warned her nephew, Richard's son, that some folk who ventured to foreign parts were niver seen ni mair! And Richard himself would sometimes express doubts that his brother would invariably survive his hair-raising escapades.

As it happened, Cherry outlived Richard by 12 years, dying in 1940, not on the horns of a charging buffalo, but of a heart-attack during a London air raid after broadcasting about his pet chimp, Toto.

In Muker church a woman was devotedly plying a vacuum cleaner as I entered. 'Ah was just wondering whether ti give up', she said, 'A lot o'dust blows in on a Set'da' '. The church records date back to 1638, and except for a gap from 1670 to 1699 they are complete to the present day.

But the church existed before that: the Bishop of Chester, then William Chadderton, consecrated it on 3 August 1580. It had a thatched roof then and the earthen floor was strewn with rushes. The pews, if any, were private ones, put in at worshippers' expense; but those who had to worship sitting on benches, or standing, were hardly likely to complain. They would remember the exhausting funeral journeys along the Corpse Way to Grinton, and be thankful that despite the conflicts that arose within the Church in Elizabeth's reign, when church building was almost at a standstill, Muker at least had its church.

While my friend finished off her cleaning I studied photographs which showed what the church looked like in bygone days. In a sense its history is the history of the dale. In the eighteenth century, lead-mining caused the population to increase until the parish numbered 1,450 souls and a bigger church was needed. It was provided in 1761, when the building was enlarged to seat 450; the walls were heightened and a new roof was made of the sort of stone flags so familiar in the Dales today.

How strange it seems that before then the roof was made of thatch! If a thatched roof were proposed now for a Dales building there would probably be an outcry of protest against such destruction of the 'character' of the dale. After the changes made in 1761, the parson preached from a three-decker pulpit to worshippers in box pews; and instead of an organ, as now, there was a musicians' platform on which sat performers on cello, violin and clarinet. What a pity *that* practice cannot be restored . . . or is it?

It certainly seems sad that in 1890 the three-decker pulpit, box pews, ceiling and gallery were all removed. Today, with all our faults, we are less prone to what seems now like change for its own sake.

A delightful representation of Swaledale scenery in stained glass is found in the east window, given in memory of a former vicar, Dr H.B. Wilson. Christ the Good Shepherd carries in his arms a lamb as he leads his flock of Swaledale sheep. Behind rises Kisdon Hill, on the left is Muker Beck, and on the right, the Swale.

'Literary Institutes' are a feature of some Dales villages. That at Muker doubles once a week, from 10.45, to 11.30 as Barclays Bank. Just how literary such institutes are today is open to question – ancient bound volumes of *Chambers' Journal* and the *Cornhill Magazine* would probably disintegrate from shock if anyone turned their pages. I dare say the billiards table was always more popular. . . .

The previous evening we had walked from Muker to Mukerside, a high point from which, surrounded by flowers, ferns and lichen-encrusted trees we could look down on the stone 'toy town' where the Keartons went to school. They, too, must have climbed up here – to see the same species of birds and to startle at every turn the young Swaledale sheep which stared in apparent terror as we confronted them on the narrow path, before racing madly past us like the half-wild things they are.

The valley, then, would be gilded by the setting sun as it was that night, touching the fields, each with its square stone barn, in the flat valley bottom; and the drystone walls enclosing staring, curious cows, their breath white, like the wreaths of misty cloud encircling the facing hills.

A few miles east of Muker is Gunnerside, named, it is said, from a

Viking chieftain, aptly, if somewhat anachronistically named Gunner, a
hero of the sagas, who probably settled here. A somewhat modernistic
representation of him adorns the sign of the King's Head inn.

Low Row, Feetham, Healaugh, Reeth. This will complete our circuit
– the lower loop of the misshapen figure 8 – that we embarked upon. The
first two villages named are almost indistinguishable from each other,
for they occupy opposite sides of the same stretch of road. But Low Row
can boast no mean distinction, for here lived Thomas Armstrong, whose
novel *Adam Brunskill* remains a worthy memorial to the days of lead-
mining. And here, too, is the inn which could tell many a tale of the
Dales – the Punch Bowl, dating at least from 1636, at which burial
parties bound for Grinton refreshed themselves while the wicker baskets
containing their dead rested forlornly in the 'dead house', the remains of
which are still to be found above Feetham.

Gunnerside, Low Row and Feetham form part of the parish of
Melbecks, an old Scandinivian work meaning 'middle beck', which
must have set many a visitor on a 'wild village chase'. There is, you see,
no village of that name: it is the designation of a parish, which, while
remaining independent, has shared its vicar with Muker since 1959. An
almost certain source, that you might think, of parochial conflict, but I
doubt if there's much squabbling: Dales folk have been taught by their
hard history to be practical and accommodating. There was squabbling
enough in the past . . . .

In 1847, while digging for gravel to make Melbecks vicarage paths, a
local man unearthed a puzzling object – a buckle of sorts, though it
belonged to no harness or belt with which he was familiar. Someone
more knowledgeable indentified it as the buckle of a sword belt and
recalled a local legend that during the Forty-Five, Dalesmen and
raiding Jacobites clashed close by – a tradition that was strengthened by
the discovery of seven or eight bodies of men apparently slain in battle.
Today, all strife forgotten, they rest in the churchyard at Low Row.

Teesdale, north of Swaledale, is no longer 'officially' in Yorkshire nor is
it even a part of the Yorkshire Dales National Park, which at some other
points transcends 'New County' boundaries. Yet it would be wrong,
surely, to exclude it from any book on the Dales.

For centuries the Tees marked Yorkshire's Northern boundary, so we
have always shared Teesdale with Durham. If we must surrender it now
(at least on paper) we can hardly be blamed for retaining an affectionate
interest in it.

Teesdale has all the variety we expect from the Dales – plus some
extra qualities: a sterner wildness, a wealth of literary associations and
the very respectable antiquity and singularity of its plant life.

Juniper trees on the hillsides could possibly trace their ancestry to pre-glacial times, and as early as the late eighteenth century it was known that rare arctic and alpine plants – mountain pansies, mountain globe flower and superb blue gentians, among many others – flourished in Upper Teesdale. It was recognised that they most probably reached their locations in the last Ice Age, flourishing in the peat bogs which formed at the edge of ice fields, but if so, how had the unique species survived to the twentieth century? Botanists throughout the world have long been interested in this question; and so, when it was first proposed in 1964 to flood part of the area to make the Cow Green Reservoir, great concern was expressed. The issue was seen as a conflict between conservation and industry and there were gloomy forecasts that, of course, industry would win.

It was then that I.C.I., as a major user of water on Teesside but one with a scientific basis and interest, stepped in with an offer of £100,000 to finance an integrated research programme investigating the whole ecology of the region. The result, after ten years, was a firm conclusion that the plants had indeed survived from the last Ice Age and the reason was to be found in the very nature of Upper Teesdale: its hard, bleak loneliness and wildness.

Greta Bridge, near the Durham market town of Barnard Castle, is a favourite starting point for explorers of Teesdale. Dickens stayed here, and Sir Walter Scott, who wrote about Rokeby Park in *Ivanhoe*. In the park itself, the Rivers Greta and Tees unite in a 'Meeting of the Waters' painted by Cotman.

Scott wrote about nearby Mortham Tower, too, a fourteenth-century fortified tower house, but long before his time another writer was at work hereabouts, though John Wyclif had perhaps little in common with Scott except industry. Born near the village of Wycliffe (on the right side of Tees, of course), he was that forerunner of Coverdale, an early translator of the Bible and a man far ahead of his time in that his object was to give every man an opportunity to form his own conclusions in religious matters.

Spreswell, the actual hamlet of his birth, exists no longer, but Egglestone Abbey, near Barnard Castle, where Wyclif was a student, remains as a gracious ruin in a lovely setting.

Equally striking is the ruin of Bowes Castle, on the road to desolate Stainmore. Its large, foursquare Norman keep, which is all that remains, stands on the site of a Roman station, Lavatrae. A more recent relic, that of the building which became 'Dotheboys Hall' in Dickens's *Nicholas Nickleby*, has possibly more popular appeal.

The old school, once a café, had been turned into flats the last time I was there. 'Amazing how many they've managed to pack into it', said a chance aquaintance on the roadside. And indeed the windows then were chintzy with curtains that would have doubtless suggested heaven to Smike and inflicted apoplexy on Squeers. I am assured, by the way, on the grounds of village tradition, that William Shaw, who ran the original 'Academy', was by no means the villain we know as Squeers. Even so, a grave in the churchyard remains as a pathetic memorial to the original of Smike.

From Bowes you may follow a good moorland road to the main Teesdale road, the 6277, and Cotherstone, where only the motte, or mound, remains of Cotherstone Castle – thanks to our Scottish friends of bygone days; though perhaps there were faults on both sides, for the Fitzhughs, who built Cotherstone in 1200 or thereabouts, had feuded with the Kerrs of Jed in Roxburghshire for generations.

More peaceable folk built the Quaker meeting house reached by field paths bordered by holly and wild roses, and buried their humble dead beneath low, identical gravestones.

A little further along the 6277 a road leads west to Hunderthwaite in the valley of the River Balder, which flows here from the wastes of Stainmore to fill enormous reservoirs. In Baldersdale lives Hannah Hauxwell, the single-handed farmer whose simple dignity won the hearts of all who watched Barry Cockcroft's television film *Too Long a Winter*, or read his consequent book *Hannah in Yorkshire*, describing a daily life so hard and primitive that he might well have been writing of an earlier century.

Hunderthwaite itself has a melancholy fame: near here in 1070 a Scottish force under King Malcolm Canmore shed much Teesdale blood.

It may well have been during the same conflict that the church of Romaldkirk, a little way north-east, was destroyed – along with so much else that when William the Conqueror came his vengeful way north, there was nothing left for him to ravage; nor could the Domesday Book commissioners find anything but 'waste' to record.

Yet today Romaldkirk's Early English church is properly proud of its title as the 'Cathedral of the Dales' and has as much right to the name as some other claimants. No less justified (if no more rare) is the long-held claim of the village itself to be a 'Gateway' – this time to the 'Alpine District' of Yorkshire. It is certainly attractive with its stone cottages around a spacious green; its pinfold and double stocks.

It takes its name, incidentally, from either St Romauld of Ravenna or the Northumbrian St Rumald, whom I must admit I much prefer: he declared at his birth 'I am a Christian', preached a noble sermon and died 'full of miracles' – when only three days old. Surely a well spent life – if short.

The road north-westward passes through Mickleton. Its name heralds the proximity of Mickle Fell, rising above the valley of the Lune, a river which is captured in the Selset and Grassholme reservoirs before it joins the Tees, east of Middleton-in-Teesdale.

The 'Capital of Upper Teesdale', Middleton makes few other claims to distinction – or to beauty – but its significance in the history of Teesdale is undeniable. In 1815 when the London Lead Company (the Quaker Company, as it was called) came here to develop a flourishing mining industry, Middleton was little different from many another village. But with Quaker zeal and due concern for their employees' welfare, the company created a 'model village' here, and though many years have passed since the last lead was mined, the dark gritstone houses, 'built on lead', and the clock tower on the 'Quaker Company's' old office building remind us that this quiet village was once a boom town.

Middleton might hope today for a different kind of 'boom' – in tourists. Most of them are bound for High Force five miles up the dale – and whether it belongs rightfully to Yorkshire or Durham, it is one of the sights of the North. Here, from a height of 50 feet the Tees plunges in white cataracts between two great rock pillars into a deep tree-girt basin, the brown of its surface flecked white with foam. My notebook records attempts to describe the noise – 'roar', 'thunder', 'growl' – and if, like me, you find them all inadequate, you must supply your own description.

Here we are on the edge of the Upper Teesdale National Nature Reserve where Mickle Fell, Yorkshire's (I insist on it) highest mountain at 2,591 feet, lords it over Cronkley Fell and Widdybank Fell. They, too, are part of the nature reserve, like Cauldron Snout – splendidly evocative name for the narrow, boiling torrent which splashes, foams and eddies for 150 yards from Cow Green Reservoir over a bed of rocks and boulders.

Bibliography

G. Douglas Bolton, *Yorkshire Revealed*, Oliver and Boyd, 1955
K.J. Bonser, *The Drovers*, Macmillan, 1970
R. Fedden & R. Joekes (editors) *The National Trust Guide*, Jonathan Cape, 1973
Edward Hart, *The Hill Shepherd*, David and Charles, 1977
Marie Hartley and Joan Ingilby, *Yorkshire Portraits*, J.M. Dent, 1961
Eric Lodge (compiler) *The Yorkshire Dales*, Yorkshire Dales Tourist Association (published annually)
Jessica Lofthouse, *Countrygoer in the Dales*, Robert Hale & Co., 1964
W.R. Mitchell, *Wild Pennines*, Robert Hale, 1976
Arthur Raistrick, *The Pennine Dales*, Eyre and Spottiswoode, 1968
Arthur Raistrick, *Old Yorkshire Dales*, David and Charles, 1967
Neil Wingate and Linden Stafford, *Grassington and Wharfedale*, 1977
G.B. Wood, *Yorkshire Villages*, Robert Hale, 1971
Geoffrey Wright, *The Yorkshire Dales*, David and Charles, 1977
Yorkshire Life files

Index

Addlebrough 125, 126
Aire Gap 28
Aire, River 20, 21, 27
Airmyn 21
Airton 21, 27
Aldborough 104-5
Alms Cliff Crag 55
Angram Reservoir 101-2
Annison, Peter and Ruth 131
Appersett 134
Appletreewick 15, 66, 67, 68
Arkengarthdale 146, 147
Arkle Beck 146
Arkle Town 147
Armstrong, Thomas 152
Arncliffe 75-6
Arthington 56-7
Askrigg 111, 123-4, 134
Atkinson, Richard 48
Austwick 15, 42
Aysgarth 120
  Falls 120

Bain, River 125, 126
Bainbridge 124-5, 126
Balder, River 154
Baldersdale 154
Bardale 125
Barden Tower 30, 65-6
Bardsey 54
  Bingley Arms 54
  Congreve, William 54
Beamsley 50
Beck Hall 24-5
Beckermonds 78
Bedale 109
Bell Busk 28
Benson, Robert 52
Bentham 42
Bishop, R. W. S. 17-18
Bishopdale 120
Bolton Castle 116, 117, 119
Bolton Hall (Wharfedale) 64
Bolton Hall (Wensleydale) 117
Bolton Percy 51
Bolton Priory 16, 26, 63-5
Booze 147
Bordley 25

Boroughbridge 104-5
  Devil's Arrows 104-5
Boston Spa 53
Bouthwaite 99
Bowen, Owen 54
Bowes 153-4
  Castle 153
Braithwaite Hall 112
Bramham Park 52-3
Brigantes 15
Briggflatts Meeting House 47
Brimham Rocks 14, 94-5
Brontë, Charlotte 31-2
Buckden 78, 120
  Pike 78, 121
Burley-in-Wharfedale 60
Burley Woodhead 60
Burnsall 67-8
Buttertubs Pass 133-4, 150

Calton 20
Calvert, Kit 127-9
Cam Houses 79, 125
Carlton 112
Carperby 15, 121
Carr, John 54-5
Castle Bolton 116, 118
Catrake Force 148-9
Catterick Camp 139
Cauldron Snout 155
Cautley Spout 47
Caves and pot-holes 39-41, 77, 101
Cawood 50, 51
Chapel-le-Dale 40
Christie, W. L. 111-12
Clapham 41
Clifford, Henry 65-6
Clifford, Lady Anne 29, 30-1, 66, 122
Clough, River 46, 48
Cockcroft, Barry 48, 154
Colsterdale 110-11
Congreve 54, 140
Constantine, Henry 112
Corpse Way 145, 150
Cotherstone 154
Cotterdale 134-5
Cotter Force 134

Countersett 126
  Hall 126
Cover, River 112
Coverdale, Miles 112, 153
Coverham 112
Cow Green Reservoir 153, 155
Cowthorpe 81-2
Crackpot 146
Cragdale 125, 127
Crakehall 109
Cromwell, Oliver 26-7, 29-31, 91, 104

Dacre Banks 94
Dales, definition of 14
Danby, William 110-11
Darnley, Lord 112
Darwin, Charles 22-3
Deadman's Hill 101
Dee, River 46
Dent 37, 45-6
  Sedgewick, Adam 45-6
Denton Hall 59
Dodd Fell 79, 127
'Dotheboys Hall' 153
Downholme 145
Druids' Temple 110-11

Easby Abbey 16, 143
Easby Church 143
East Witton 112
Eden, River 47
Edward IV 113
Egglestone Abbey 153
Eldroth 42
Ellerton Priory 145

Fairfax, Admiral Robert 53
Fairfax family 59
Fairfax, Thomas 51, 59-60, 87
Farnley Hall 24, 59
Farnley, Walter 24
Farrer, Reginald 42
Fawkes, Guy 82
Feetham 146, 152
Fleet Moss 79
Fothergill, John 125-6
Fountaine, Richard 69
Fountains Abbey 16, 22, 25, 26, 77, 94,
  106-7
Fountains Fell 38, 40
Fox, George 42-3, 47
Foxup 75, 77

Gargrave 28, 39
Garsdale 44, 48, 115, 133
Gayle 131-2
Giggleswick 42-4
  Ebbing and Flowing Well 43-4
Goldsborough Hall 82
Gordale Beck 24
Gordale Scar 20, 23-4
Gouthwaite Reservoir 16, 98, 99-100,
  101
Grassington 71-4, 97
Great Pinseat 147
Great Shunner 127, 133, 134

Green Dragon Inn 132
Greenhow 97-8
Greta Bridge 153
Grinton 134, 145
Grisedale 48-9
Gunnerside 146, 151-2

Hambleton Hill 100
Hampsthwaite 16, 92-3
  Amy Woodforde-Finden 92, 93
  Jane Ridsdale 93
  Peter Barker 92, 93
  William M. Thackeray 92, 93
Hanlith 27
Hardraw 132-3, 134
  Hardraw Force 132-3
Harewood 54-6
  Castle 56
  Church 56
  Earl of 56
  Harewood House 54, 55-6
  Princess Royal 56
Harrogate 88-91
  Churches 90
  Pump Room 89
  Pump Room Museum 90
  Royal Baths 89
  Royal Hall 90
  Tewit Well 89
  Valley Gardens 89
  Wells 89, 90
Halton Gill 77
Hawes 127-131, 150
Hawkswick 75, 76
Haworth 32
Hazlewood Castle 52, 53
Healaugh 146, 152
Hetton 20, 28
High Force 155
High Seat 149
Horsehouse 112
Horton-in-Ribblesdale 38, 39
How Stean 100
Howgill Fells 46
Howitt, William 45
Hunderthwaite 154

Ilkley 62-3
Ilkley Moor 29, 61-2
  'Ilkla' Moor baht 'at' 61-2
  Churches 62
  Cow and Calf Rocks 29, 62
  Manor House 63
  White Wells 62
Ingilby family 91
Ingleborough 15, 38-9, 41
Ingleborough Hall 41, 42
Ingleton 37, 41

Jervaulx Abbey 16, 111-12

Kearton, Cherry and Richard 149-50
Keasden 42
Keighley 32
  East Riddlesden Hall 32-3
Keld 146, 148-9

Kettlewell 77, 112, 121
Ketyll, Dame Alice 41
Kidstones Pass 120
Kildwick 32
Kilnsey Crag 74-5
Kingsley, Charles 22, 23, 75, 115
Kirk Hammerton 82
Kirkby Malham 25-7
Kirkby Malzeard 100
Kirklington 108
Kisdon Force 148-9
Kisdon Hill 134, 148
Knaresborough 84-9
  Blind Jack 82-3, 84, 86
  Castle 87
  Dropping Well 84, 88
  Eugene Aram 84, 85-6, 99
  Fort Montague 88
  Mother Shipton 84-5, 88
  St Robert 88
  St Robert's Cave 85, 88
  St Robert's Chapel 88

Lambert, Major General 27
Lammerside Castle 47-8
Langcliffe 35, 37-8
Langstrothdale 78
Langstrothdale Chase 50, 78
Langthwaite 146
Lascelles, Edwin 58
Lawkland 42
Lawson, Fred and Muriel 116, 118
Lead Church 52
Lead-mining 146-7
Leyburn 115-16
Leyburn Shawl 116
Linton 68-70
Little Stainforth 42
Litton 76, 77
Littondale 50, 75-7
Lofthouse 85, 96, 100
Long Marston 81
Long Preston 34
Lothersdale 31-2
Lovely Seat 127, 133, 149
Low Row 145, 152
  Punch Bowl Inn •145
Lunds 135

Malham 16, 24-5, 74
  Cove 20, 21-2, 23
  Tarn 20, 21, 22
Malhamdale 21-8
Mallerstang 48
Marmion Tower 107
Markenfield Hall 105-6
Marrick Priory 145
Marsett 127
Marske 144
Marston Moor, Battle of 81, 91
Mary, Queen of Scots 116, 122
Masham 109-10
Masham, Lord 110
Mastiles Lane 74
Melbecks 152
Metcalfe Family 121-3

Metcalfe, Jack (hornblower) 124
Mewith Head 42
Mickleton 154
Mickle Fell 38, 154, 155
Mid-Craven Fault 20, 36
Middleham 113-15
  Castle 113-15
  Church 115
Middleton-in-Teesdale 155
Moorcock Inn 48
Morrison, Walter 16, 22, 23, 27
Muker 16, 134, 146, 149, 150-1, 152

Nappa Hall 121-3
Neville, Archbishop George 51
Neville family 108, 113-15
Newby Hall 105
Newton Kyme Hall 53
Nidd, River 80 et seq
Norber Boulders 14-15, 42
Nostell Priory 58
Nun Appleton 51, 60
Nun Monkton 80, 81

Otley 50, 57-9
  Chevin 57, 58
  Chippendale, Thomas 54, 58-9
  Old Grammar School 58
  Prince Henry's Grammar School 57
  Show 57
Ouse, River 50, 51
'Owd Bartle' 119-20
'Owd Man' 97-8

Parcevall Hall 66
Park Rash 77, 112-13
Parr, Catherine 108
Pateley Bridge 96-7
Pendragon Castle 48
Penhill 119, 120
Penyghent 38, 39
Plumpton Rocks 84
Pockstones Moor 59
Punchbowl Inn 145, 152

Ramsgill 85, 96, 98-9, 100
Rawthey, River 46, 47, 48-9
Raydale 125
Redmire 117-18
Reeth 143, 144-5, 146, 152
  Folk Museum 144-5
Ribblehead 40
Ribble, River 34 et seq
Ribston Hall 82
Richard III, King 113-15
Richmond 136-44
  Castle 136-8, 139-40
  Frances I'Anson 142
  Georgian Theatre 140-2
  Green Howards 138-9
  Holy Trinity Church 138
  King Olav of Norway 138-9
  Potter Thompson 137-8
  Powell, Lord Baden 139
  'Prisoners of Conscience' 139-40
Riley, William 38

Ripley   91
Ripon   15, 103-4
    Cathedral   103-4
    Corn Bell   104
    Hornblower   104
    St Wilfrid's Feast   103
    Unicorn Hotel   104
Rogan's Seat   147, 149
Rokeby Park   153
Romaldkirk   154
Ropemaking   131
Roses, Wars of   51-2, 113
Rudding Park   84
Rylstone   28
Ryther   51

Salt, Sir Titus   21
Saltaire   20-1
Scar House Reservoir   96, 101-2
Scrope family   118-19, 122
Sedbergh   46-7
Sedbergh School   125
Sedgwick, Adam   45-6
Semerdale   125-7
Semerwater   15, 16, 20, 125, 126-7
Senior, Job   60-1
sett suffix   127
Settle   34-7
    Castleberg Crag   36
    Dr George Birkbeck   36, 43
    Naked Man   35
    Pig Yard Club and Museum   35, 36
    Preston's Folly   36
    Settle-Carlisle Railway   36-7, 40, 45
    Shambles   36
    Tot Lord   35
    Victoria Cave   35, 38
Shipton, Mother   50-1, 84-5
Skipton   28-31
    Castle   28-31
    Church   31
    Corn Mill   31
    Craven Museum   31
Skirfare, River   75
Snape Castle   108-9
Spennithorne   116
Spofforth Castle   83-4
Stake Pass   127
Stainforth   38
Stainmore   153, 154
Stalling Busk   126-7
Starbotton   77-8, 112, 121
Strid, The   65
Stump Cross Caverns   97-8
Stillman, Edward   149
Sutcliffe, Halliwell   68, 69, 70

'Swaledale Royal'   148
Swale, River   136, 137
Swinithwaite   119
Swinton Castle   110

Tadcaster   53
Tan Hill   39, 146, 147-8
Teesdale   152-5
Thoralby   120
Thornton in Lonsdale   44
Thorpe-in-the-Hollow   68
Three Peaks   38-9, 79
Threshfield   70-1
Thruscross Reservoir   59
Thwaite   16, 133, 134, 146, 149-50
Tockwith   81
Towton, Battle of   51-2, 66, 83
Trollers Ghyll   66
Trow Gill   41
Turner, J.M.W.   24, 59

Ulleskelf   51

Vavasour family   52, 53

Walburn Hall   145-6
Walden Beck   120, 121
Waldendale   120-1
Warwick, Earl of   51, 113
Washburn, River   59
Washburn Valley   59
Wath   96, 99, 108
Well   107-8
Wensley   116-17, 118
    Church   116-17
Wensleydale cheese   128-9
West Burton   120, 121
West End Church   59
West Scrafton   112
West Tanfield   107, 108
West Witton   119-20
Wetherby   53-4
Whernside   38-9, 40
Whernside, Great   101, 102, 112
Whernside, Little   101, 112
Whitcliffe Scar   143-4
Winterburn   20, 28
Wolsey, Cardinal   50-1
Wyclif   112, 153
Wycliffe   112, 153

Yockenthwaite   15, 16, 78
Yorke's Folly   96-7, 100
Yorkshire Dales National Park   13, 14, 16
Yorkshire Naturalists' Trust   23